STUDIES IN THE CARTESIAN PHILOSOPHY

STUDIES

IN THE

CARTESIAN PHILOSOPHY

BY

NORMAN SMITH, M.A.

LECTURER AT QUEEN MARGARET COLLEGE, AND ASSISTANT TO THE
PROFESSOR OF LOGIC, IN THE UNIVERSITY OF GLASGOW

NEW YORK

RUSSELL & RUSSELL · INC

1962

L. C. CATALOG CARD NO: 62—8404

PRINTED IN THE UNITED STATES OF AMERICA

PREFACE.

WHEN Huxley declares that Descartes advanced beyond his age and anticipated what would be the thoughts of all men three hundred years after him, he has mainly in view Descartes' achievements in the natural sciences. And in that relation the assertion is undoubtedly justified. In a more adequate manner than even Galileo or Bacon, Descartes formulated the methods and defined the ideals of modern science. A very different estimate must, however, be made of his work in metaphysics. Though the new and definite conception of nature which he derived from his studies in the sciences, enabled him to state the problem of perception, and the problem of the relation of mind and body, much in the form in which they persist to the present day, his metaphysical teaching is perverted, I shall try to show, by principles wholly at variance with his own positive scientific views. If the interpretation which I give of Descartes' philosophy be correct, it is no exaggeration to assert that all that lies outside his philosophy of nature, or is not illumined by a reflex light from it, remains in essentials scholastic in conception.

My original intention, therefore, was to dwell chiefly upon Descartes' philosophy of the sciences as the really important part of his system; but realising more and more fully as I proceeded in my study of the subject, how very artificial is the connection between his metaphysics and his scientific views, I came to the conclusion that separate treatment of them would be advisable. His philosophy of nature I have reserved for future consideration, and in this present volume limit myself, as far as possible, to his metaphysics. I first examine his metaphysical principles as they appear in his own writings; and then, by tracing their influence on the thinking of his successors, seek to determine further their implications and consequences.

If we except the late Professor Veitch's volume of translations, the preface of which is written from a point of view no longer generally received, there

is but one English work—that of Professor Mahaffy
in the Blackwood Philosophical Series—exclusively
devoted to Descartes. And as Professor Mahaffy's
book is mainly biographical, I consider that no
apology is required for this attempt to examine in
detail the principles of the Cartesian Philosophy.
I may add that though this volume is not designed
to be an introduction to the study of Descartes, I
have throughout presupposed only such knowledge
of the period as may be gained from any history
of philosophy. I may specially refer the reader to
that section of Kuno Fischer's history, which has
been translated into English under the title, *Descartes
and His School.*

To the late Professor Adamson I am indebted
both for guidance in the literature of the subject
and for assistance in special difficulties. On one
point in particular, viz., Descartes' view of time and
its significance in his metaphysics, I received from
him invaluable suggestions of which I have sought
to make good use. In the autumn of last year
Professor Adamson read through my manuscript
and made several important criticisms. Professor
Henry Jones and Professor A. S. Pringle Pattison
have rendered me the same service, and for

their comments, by which my book has greatly profited, I am most grateful. My thanks are also due to my friend, Mr. William Menzies, for reading the proofs of the whole book.

September, 1902.

CONTENTS.

CHAPTER I.

CHAPTER II.

CHAPTER III.

CHAPTER V.

CHAPTER VI.

CHAPTER VII.

CHAPTER I.

THE PROBLEM OF DESCARTES.

WITH Descartes philosophy made a fresh start: a new set of problems had arisen, and it is as the first to face these problems that he has been called "the father of modern philosophy." To comprehend his position we must see how, from causes only in part themselves philosophical, a new view of the self and a new view of nature had grown up, demanding a reconsideration of the problem of knowledge.

If we seek to characterize the point of view of the Greek philosophers, it would probably, on the whole, be true to assert that for them man and nature are inwardly related. The soul, Aristotle teaches, realises itself in and through the body. Matter and form, the material and the immaterial, are two aspects involved in all natural existences, and are separable only by abstraction. Descartes' attitude, on the other hand, is wholly different. Those aspects of reality, which Aristotle in distinguishing reconciles, are by Descartes held apart as absolute opposites. Between man and nature, between soul and body, there is, on Descartes' view, no internal kinship. The mind does not spread itself over the body so as to become materialised, nor does the body through a vital force become spiritualised. And the human body being, therefore, as purely material as any other object in space, its conjunction with the immaterial soul must be regarded as an ultimate fact, explicable only as due to the arbitrary will of God. The most absolute spiritualism is made to complement an equally extreme materialism. Souls are conceived as scattered points of life in a universe of dead matter.

To trace this change of mental outlook in its growth, and adequately to determine its causes, would involve a history of the whole period from Aristotle to Descartes, and we can therefore do no more than name the main influences which brought it about. Speaking very roughly, it was in Stoicism and through Christianity that the antagonism between man and nature came to be felt. Through the Christian conception of the value of each human soul, the individual was separated out from the cosmic whole, and given an independent reality and worth. Attention was turned more to morality and to the inner life, as distinguished from the outward, purely social, civic life of the Greeks. With the passing of the Greek civilization, men, we may say, became hermits; and consciousness, defeating its own ends, formed an inner world, independent of, and even antagonistic to, the outer world. This tendency towards subjectivity was highly developed by the fourth century A.D., and we need not, therefore, be surprised to find quite explicit in Augustine the *cogito ergo sum* of Descartes. A mere list of the problems upon which Augustine wrote treatises—divine grace and individual sin, predestination and the freedom of the will[1]—reveals the break that has meantime taken place with Greek modes of thought. As his treatment of the problem of knowledge, in its emphasis on the subjectivity of the process, is equally modern, and strangely similar to that of Descartes, it will repay us to dwell upon it at length.

---

[1] All of these are problems foreign to the Greek mind. Augustine's *Confessions* also form the first instance of what is an entirely modern form of literature, autobiography.

Augustine runs the problem of knowledge back into three mysteries, which he recognizes as being for him altogether insoluble. The first of these is how the unextended mind can contain images of an extended world. Though the mind, in contrast to the body, is unextended, it is not so in the sense of being *out* of space, for being finite it is always located at a particular point *in* space. It is out of space only in the sense of being a mathematical point in it,[1] not of being free from all the limitations of it. Now since the mind has thus its own position in space, it cannot any more than a material body go outside its own boundaries—all the more so, as Augustine's friend Evodius would say, that it is not big enough to have boundaries. All knowledge must be in and through knowledge

---

[1] How small, Augustine notes, is the pupil of the eye which yet illumines the whole heavens above us. The eye, too, of the eagle, though yet smaller, is far more powerful, which shows that size has nothing to do with the power of perception. Well, therefore, may the mind, which can contain in image not only the whole heavens, but innumerable immense spaces, be but a point (*De Quantitate Animae*, cap. xiv.). And, indeed, the point is of all existences in space the best and most powerful. *In* it the line begins and *in* it ends, line intersects line *through* it, the angle is formed *by* it, and *by* it also, as centre, the direction of every part of that most perfect figure, the circle, is regulated (*De Quant. An.* cap. xii.).

of the self, and if bodies outside it are to be known by it, that can only be by there appearing in it representations of them.[1] The doctrine of representative perception is thus already full-blown in Augustine. Knowledge is a subjective process going on separately in the mind of each individual. "Each sees one thing in himself such that another person may believe what he says of it, yet may not see it."[2] And it is as a consequence of this doctrine of representative perception that Augustine formulates the *cogito ergo sum* as the sole immediate certainty. "We both are, and know that we are, and delight in our being, and our knowledge of it. Moreover, in these three things no true-seeming

[1] Cf. Malebranche, *Recherche de la Verité*, liv. III., pt. II., chap. I., p. 377. (Our references throughout are to Jules Simon's edition of Malebranche's works.) "Our minds cannot issue out of the body in order to measure the magnitude of the heavens, and in consequence cannot see external objects save by the ideas that represent them. To this everyone must agree." Cf. *Ibid.* p. 373. "We see the sun, the stars and an infinity of objects outside us ; and it is not likely that the soul issues from the body, and goes, so to speak, wandering in the heavens in order to contemplate there all these objects (qu'elle aille, pour ainsi dire, se promener dans les cieux pour y contempler tous ces objets)." Cf. Descartes, *Les Passions de l'Ame*, art. 33.

[2] *De Trinitate*, lib. IX., cap. VI. Eng. trans. (ed. by Dods), p. 231.

illusion disturbs us; for we do not come into
contact with these by some bodily sense, as we
perceive the things outside of us—colours, *e.g.* by
seeing, sounds by hearing, smells by smelling, tastes
by tasting, hard and soft objects by touching—of
all which sensible objects it is the images resembling
them, but not themselves which we perceive in the
mind, and hold in the memory, and which excites
us to desire the objects. But, without any delusive
representation of images or phantasms, I am most
certain that I am, and that I know and delight in
this. In respect of these truths I am not at all
afraid of the Academicians, who say, What if you
are deceived? For if I am deceived, I am. For
he who is not, cannot be deceived; and if I am
deceived, by this same token I am. And since I
am if I am deceived, how am I deceived in believing
that I am? for it is certain that I am if I am
deceived."[1]

Augustine saw no difficulty in admitting that
bodies, by acting on the senses, produce images of
themselves in the mind. The problem, as it presented
itself to him, rather was how if, as is inevitable,
the images so produced conform to the nature of

---

[1] *De Civitate Dei*, lib. XI., cap. XXVI. Eng. trans., pp. 468-9.

the unextended mind in which they appear, they
can yet be images of, and so afford knowledge of,
the extended.   That is the problem over which he
puzzled to the end, with the full consciousness that
it was for him insoluble.   There is in the mind a
certain wonderful power (*mira quaedam vis*) by
which it can contain *tanta coeli, terrae, marisque
spatia*.[1]

It is true that at times Augustine resorts to a
vague mystic solution of the difficulty, assuming that
the mind is capable of overcoming spatial differences, and of being in many places at once—at
once present in the bodily eye perceiving, and also
present to the external distant object perceived.
But so long as space is regarded as real outside
the mind, and the physiological standpoint is maintained in explanation of the origin of knowledge,
such a view is meaningless.   The really valuable
part of Augustine's teaching lies in his emphasis
on the necessity of taking the mind as unextended,
and yet as located in the extended.

The second mystery, which impressed Augustine,
is how mind can know external objects, and yet

[1] *De Quant. An.* cap. XIV.   Cf. *Confessionum*, lib. X. cap.
VIII.-XVI.

be ignorant of those internal parts of the body with which it is in immediate connection. "This is a very important question which I now ask, Why have I no need of science to know that there is a sun in the heavens, and a moon, and all the other stars; but must have the aid of science in order to know, on moving my finger whence the act begins—with my heart, or my brain, or with both, or with neither; why I do not require a teacher to know what is so far above me; but must wait for someone else to learn whence that is done by me which is done within me? . . . How is it that, while we can count our limbs externally, even in the dark and with closed eyes, by the bodily sense which is called 'the touch,' we know nothing of our internal functions in the very central region of the soul itself, where that power is present which imparts life [and sensation to the body],—a mystery this which, I apprehend, no medical man of any kind, whether empirics, or anatomists, or dogmatists, or methodics (*methodicos*), or any man living, have any knowledge of."[1]

[1] *De Anima et ejus Origine*, lib. IV. cap. VI. (Eng. trans. p. 305.)

The third mystery, which is obviously connected with the above, is the complement of the truth that self-consciousness is the essence of mind. "Neither the heaven of heavens, nor the measure of the stars, nor the scope of sea and land, nor the nethermost hell [are the tests of our incapacity]; it is our own selves whom ourselves are incapable of comprehending; it is our own selves who, in our too great height and strength, transcend the humble limits of our own knowledge; it is our own selves whom we are incapable of embracing, although we are certainly not outside ourselves."[1] "We often assume that we shall retain a thing in our memory and so thinking, we do not write it down. But afterwards, when we wish to recall it, it refuses to come to mind; and we are then sorry that we thought it would return to memory, or that we did not secure it in writing so as to prevent its escape; when lo, on a sudden, without our seeking it, it occurs to us. . . . Now how does it happen that I knew not how we are abstracted from, and denied to, ourselves; and similarly are ignorant how we are restored and reproduced to ourselves? . . . For where do we make our quest, except in

[1] *Ibid.* (Eng. trans. p. 306.)

our own selves? And what is it we search for,
except our own selves? . . . Do you not observe,
even with alarm, so deep a mystery? And what is all
this but our own nature—not what it has been, but
such as it now is? And observe how much wider
the question is than our comprehension thereof."[1]

Now the advance from Augustine to Descartes,
and the deepening of the problem in Descartes,
consists just in this, that while these three problems
remain, and remain at bottom as insoluble for
Descartes[2] as for Augustine, there has arisen,
through the growth of a scientific view of matter
the further problem, how soul and body can possibly interact, and how, therefore, the latter can
produce sensations in the mind. Like the Scholastics
after him, Augustine despised physical science as of
no use for the attaining of the soul's salvation.
What he alone sought was knowledge of God and
of the self. *Deum et animam scire cupio. Nihilne
plus? Nihil omnino.*[3] And it was at least eight

---

[1] *Ibid.* cap. VII. (Eng. trans. p. 307.) Cf. *Confessionum,*
lib. X. cap. VIII.

[2] Augustine does not seem to have exercised any direct
influence upon Descartes. Nevertheless, these problems inevitably reappeared in Descartes' philosophy.

[3] *Soliloquiorum,* lib. I. cap. II.

centuries before nature, through the love of her in
the arts, and the study of her in the sciences,
could become the second reality, at once the
opposite and the complement of mind, and so one
further step be made in the problem of knowledge.
The Renascence philosophers, however, in their
reaction against the theological view of nature as
the principle of evil, went to the other extreme,
and blurred its features by spiritualising it. It was
a return to the Greek point of view, and so far a
gain, a gain too in the restored respect for natural
science ; but the mathematical sciences had, through
Galileo and Descartes, to speak more clearly, before
the specifically modern theory of nature could be
possible. In the sharply outlined dualism of
Descartes there is a plastic clearness that is in as
great contrast to the mystic pantheism, all things
interfused, of the Renascence thinkers, as to the
Aristotelian physics of the Schools.

It is by the all-important rôle ascribed to motion
that the Cartesian physics distinguishes itself from
Greek science.[1]   Matter is perfectly homogeneous,

[1] Descartes' views we state, on this and the following pages,
very summarily. They will be developed at length in chapters
II. and III.

and wholly passive: an inert continuous mass, it cannot in any essential way be distinguished, either by positive or by negative predicates, from the space which it fills. It is, indeed, capable of figure, but such differences of figure are due to motion, and depend on its continuance. Motion is the sole differentiating factor in nature, for it is it alone that breaks up the inert continuous mass into the different 'kinds' of material 'atoms,' and that, by impelling them one against the other, gives rise alike to the heavens and to the earth with all that they contain. "Give me," says Descartes, "matter and motion, and I shall construct the universe." In nature one single event, motion in space, infinitely diversified with itself, alone takes place. All the manifold qualitative differences, that appear to be revealed by the senses, are the original creation of mind, and by it projected out into the external world.

Nature is thus not merely dehumanised but also despiritualised, and becomes the direct opposite of the mind. All that is asserted of the one must be denied of the other. Matter is extended, infinitely divisible, purely passive: mind is unextended, in-divisible, active. Matter as being in space has all its parts external to one another: mind as being out

of space has its whole content within itself. Each
extended thing is dependent on what is beyond
it: the self is independent of all else, and self-
sufficient. This dualism has been named the
Cartesian dualism, not because Descartes invented
or discovered it, but simply because in him it
gained its most thorough and perfect expression.
It was involved in the scientific and general thought
of his time, and to it, as the then ascertainable
truth about the self and nature, he had to adapt
his thinking. He starts from this dualism, and his
special metaphysical problem is to determine how
under these conditions knowledge is possible. If
the spiritual world and the material world are in
absolute antagonism, how is the *fact* of knowledge,
a fact which involves their interrelation, their inter-
penetration, to be accounted for? How can a
material world be known by an immaterial mind?

Like Augustine, Descartes regards the finite unextended mind as set into an infinitely extended
material world, and fixed down always to a particular locality in it, namely, to the brain, along with
which it moves to and fro in space. Without
thought that any other was possible, he took up
this physiological attitude, and doing so had no

option but also to adopt the doctrine of representative perception. The self can know nothing but its own states, and only indirectly by an inference from them establish the existence of any other being. Hence the utter misrepresentation of the internal dialectic of Descartes' thought, if we start, as Descartes himself does, with the *cogito ergo sum* as the really ultimate element in his system. The *cogito ergo sum* is simply one consequence of the doctrine of representative perception, which is itself a consequence of his dualistic starting-point.

But inevitable though the doctrine of representative perception be as a consequence of Descartes' dualism, as a solution of the problem of knowledge it is a total failure. The problem is merely pushed further back. Since ideas are regarded as the objects of mind, and as exact copies of what exists outside mind, all those activities and processes, which the term 'idea' was originally invented to express, have to be thrown back into a mind supposed to lie behind them, and the problem how the mind can know anything, be it only a mental image,[1] is not so much as considered.

---

[1] And surely that is as great and as real a problem as how the mind should know a material body, for all the character-

Even granting, however, the admissibility of thus regarding knowledge as consisting in the observation by a mind of images within it, the new and scientific view of matter throws special difficulties in the way of such a doctrine; for sense-perceptions can no longer be regarded either as caused by the external objects or as copies of them. The time-honoured theory that material bodies are known by way of the sense-organs ceases to have any meaning. Since the sense-organs are parts of the extended organism, they are as material as anything else, and therefore the assertion, that bodies are known by way of them, amounts to no more than the absurdity of saying that bodies become known to mind by acting on other bodies. Also, if this theory be taken as meaning that sensations are due to the action of the *brain* on the *mind*, it is contradicted by the fact that, while the only form of action conceivable in matter is impact, no impact can be given to the

istics of the external object are to be found in the image that copies it, not excepting, as Augustine insists, its extendedness. Saving the local difference between mind and external object, there is not one difficulty that is removed by naming the image 'mental.' Even the mind 'though very closely united to itself' need not on that account, as Malebranche observes, be known by itself.

immaterial.   All that takes place in the brain is motion of its material particles.   These vibrations can obviously neither transform themselves into sensations, nor, while remaining as they are, hand over to the mind sensations ready-made.   Descartes is therefore forced to regard all sensations as innate in mind, and as produced by it out of itself.

Then, secondly, these sense-perceptions cannot be regarded as images of external objects.   The visual image, for instance, of an object is coloured, whereas the external object is colourless.   And what thus holds of the secondary qualities is likewise true of the primary.   We find in the mind, to use Descartes' own illustration,[1] two wholly diverse ideas of the sun : the one idea, the sense-image, by which the sun appears extremely small, seems to come to us directly from the sun through the senses ; the other idea, whereby it is represented as many times larger than the whole earth, we have constructed for ourselves in physical science.   These two ideas cannot both resemble the same sun, and reason teaches us

---

[1] *Meditations*, III. (Cousin's edition, I. p. 271) ; Veitch's trans. p. 120.   As only the first three volumes of the new edition of Descartes' works have been published, our references throughout are to Cousin's edition.

that the one which is given us in sense, and which
seems to have immediately emanated from the sun,
is the most unlike. The true nature of the sun, as
it exists without us, is thus revealed not by sense
but by thought. Our sense-images are but pictures
in our minds, and do not represent, but misrepresent,
the true nature of the real. There are two external
worlds, the one rich with its bright variety of
diverse qualities, appearing to the 'senses,' the other,
poverty-stricken, constituted only of matter and
motion, and discovered by the understanding.

Now, it might be expected that Descartes, when
driven by his physical theories to make this distinction, would in the ordinary way assume that the
mind by a 'faculty of thought' constructs for itself
out of the materials of sense a conception of the
real. But it is not so. The conceptions, by which
we grasp the real, are not, in Descartes' view,
activities whereby mind apprehends the non-mental,
but, like sense-images, objects which it contemplates
within itself. Also they are not derived from the
perceptions, but wholly distinct from them in nature,
resemble them only in being likewise innate. By
this strange opposition of conceptions to perceptions,
which he makes to be absolute, Descartes aggra-

vates the difficulties, already great enough in all truth, of his dualism, and lands himself, founder though he be of the physical sciences, in a rationalism more extreme in its antagonism to sense-experience than even the idealism of Plato. The causes leading Descartes to this position are to be found in his absorbing interest in the mathematical sciences, whose method he misconceived.

CHAPTER II.

THE METHOD OF DESCARTES.[1]

DESCARTES in the *Discourse* states his method in four short rules, with little explanation of how the reader is to interpret them, and for a more adequate treatment of it we must look to his earlier and less famous work, *Regulae ad Directionem Ingenii.*[2]

We may start from his second rule, which runs as follows : "We must attend only to those objects of which our mind is capable of acquiring knowledge that is certain and indubitable."[3] Trivial and commonplace as that rule appears, we might almost deduce from it Descartes' whole philosophy. The reason why he turned to philosophy is, he tells us, because his experience was a patchwork of true and

[1] In this chapter, as throughout, we have in view only Descartes' metaphysics, and hence do not dwell on his method in its relation to his work in mathematics and physics.

[2] First published, fifty years after his death, in 1701.

[3] *Reg.* II. (Cousin's edition, XI. p. 204).

false, a mass of merely probable truths, opinion not knowledge.   The *raison d'être* of philosophy lies in its attempt to carry us over from probability to knowledge, and if it fails to do that, it fails altogether.   " He who doubts much is no wiser than he who has never thought."

But further, since an assertion of probability can be made only on a basis of indubitable fact, the existence of probable knowledge proves that there also exist some absolutely certain truths.   Take the familiar instance of the die.   The probability of its falling, say, with the four up is one to six, and rests on the knowledge that the die has six sides, and that there is no special reason in the die itself why it should fall on one side rather than another. Should these facts, and the laws of arithmetic according to which we calculate the probability from them, be doubtful, the probability would cease to hold.   Possibility and probability rest on certainty, and hence can only follow it, cannot precede it.   At least a minimum of absolutely certain indubitable knowledge must be possessed by all, in order that ordinary experience, that patchwork of true and false, be possible.

" We reject, then, according to this rule, all knowledge that is only probable, and assume as a principle that we should trust only to those truths which are certain, and of which no one can doubt." [1] But, it is at once objected, that leaves us with nothing but a petty pedantic philosophy ; all that has complexity and magnitude outstrips the mind ; and hence all science that is of worth can be but probable tentative knowledge. The learned under this prejudice, Descartes repeats over and over again, have neglected the simple indubitable truths as too easy and within the reach of all. "Yet I assure them that there is a greater number of such truths than they think, and that they suffice to demonstrate firmly a multitude of propositions, as to which they have hitherto been able to express only probable opinions." [2] Those truths that are so simple and universal and indubitable that no one can be ignorant of them, just those apparently trivial and worthless truths, are the springs of knowledge. [3]

[1] *Reg.* II. (XI. p. 205).
[2] *Reg.* II. (XI. p. 205).
[3] Cf. *Reg.* IX. (XI. pp. 249-51). "It is a common failing among men to regard the most difficult things as the finest, and the majority believe they gain no new knowledge, when they discover a very clear and very simple solution of their difficulties, while they admire the subtle and profound doctrines of the philosophers, although they frequently rest on grounds that on

The method whereby the indubitable may be separated out from the doubtful, Descartes discovers in a very simple manner. "All the sciences united are nothing but the human understanding, which remains one and the same however varied be the objects to which it applies itself, and which is no more altered than is the light of the sun by the variety of the objects it illumines."[1] That is, the activities are one and the same in the construction of all knowledge, and hence from any bit of true knowledge the universal nature of the intelligence which constructed it can be discovered. Now, in mathematics we have true knowledge, and therefore by separating off in the mathematical method what is due solely to the special nature of its subject-

one has ever sufficiently verified: foolish admiration that prefers darkness to the light. . . . This is a point on which I would here insist more than on all others : namely, that every one be firmly persuaded that it is not from the great and difficult, but only from what is most simple and most easy that we must deduce even the most recondite sciences." That point of view is characteristic of all the great thinkers of the 17th and 18th centuries, who in their reaction against the mediaeval Gothic spirit hated obscurity, and misty or mystic vagueness of outline, more than aught else. Pascal has, in words strikingly similar to those of Descartes, given classical expression to this attitude in his *Pensées* (Havet, ii. pp. 307-8).

[1] *Reg.* i. (xi. p. 202).

matter, what we shall have left in our hands will
be the expression of the essence of mind in all
its purity and universality, a complete analysis of
the light whereby objects are revealed to us. It is
with that high end in view that Descartes sets
himself to examine the method of the mathematical
sciences.

But before we proceed further, let us try to discover why for Descartes the problem of method is
so all-important. He returns again and again to
the point, until we almost grow weary of his repeated
assertions that the supreme question for philosophy
is that of method; for after all, we naturally think,
is not method but the scaffolding, a means truly of
attaining knowledge, but not meant to monopolise
our attention? So long as that is our feeling, we
are still very far from a true understanding of the
position of Descartes.

In the first place, it is not true that the method
is merely an instrument for constructing knowledge.
Rather, as appears from what has just been said, it
expresses the innermost essence of mind; and the
problem of method is therefore identical with the
problem as to the nature and limits of knowledge.
Since in the method we have a complete analysis of

the mind, in determining that method we necessarily also determine the measure and scope of mind. " No question is more important than this of knowing what human knowledge is, and how far it extends; that is why we unite this double inquiry [that of method and that of the limits of knowledge] in a single question that we think ought to be examined before all others . . . ; it is an inquiry which everyone who loves truth, be it ever so little, ought to make once in his life, since it contains the true organon of knowledge and the whole of method." [1]

Secondly, Descartes declares that " we can know nothing [even of what is within our reach] until we know intelligence, since the knowledge of all things depends on it, and not it on that knowledge." [2] Though mathematical science existed before the nature of the intelligence was discovered, that was only possible through the prior discovery by the Ancients of the intelligence in a concrete form,[3] the analytical method of the Greeks being just the one true method specialised in its application to number and extension.   And, as an historical fact, only in

[1] *Reg.* VIII. (XI. pp. 245-6).
[2] *Reg.* VIII. (XI. p. 243).
[3] *Reg.* IV. (XI. pp. 217-8, 220-4).

these mathematical sciences was any knowledge of perfect certainty attained.

Thirdly, there is a statement, which Descartes twice repeats in the *Regulae*, which throws much light on this point, viz. that it is impossible to make a false inference.[1] What he means would seem to be this. It is want of data, or want of right arrangement of the data, that causes bad reasoning, never the failure to draw the true inference from what is actually before the mind.[2] To draw a conclusion that does not follow from the data considered would be for thought to break in two. The laws of identity and non-contradiction are not, as logicians assert, regulative merely, but belonging to the unchangeable essence of mind, not to its accidents, are therefore obeyed in equal perfection by all men. And that phrase gives us the key to Descartes' strange doctrine, jestingly stated, but seriously designed, at the opening of the *Discourse on Method*: "Good sense is, of all things

[1] *Reg.* II. III. (XI. pp. 207-8, 212).

[2] What we mean by a false inference is an inference out of place. We reason falsely when we make one inference and think we have made another. The fault lies always in the falsity or inadequacy of the data—in the matter, that is, and never in the form of reasoning. The inference drawn from such data, though correctly following from them, will be a false inference in the circumstances.

among men, the most equally distributed; for every
one thinks himself so abundantly provided with it,
that those even who are the most difficult to satisfy
in everything else, do not usually desire a larger
measure of this quality than they already possess.
And in this it is not likely that all are mistaken:
the conviction is rather to be held as testifying that
the power of judging aright and of distinguishing
truth from error, which is properly what is called
good sense or reason, is by nature equal in all men.
. . . For inasmuch as reason is that alone which constitutes us men, and distinguishes us from the brutes,
I am disposed to believe that it is to be found complete in each individual; and on this point to adopt
the common opinion of philosophers, who say that
the difference of greater and less holds only among
the *accidents*, and not among the *forms* or *natures* of
individuals of the same *species*." Since all men, as
rational beings, are alike in the power of perceiving
rational connection, the capacity for procuring and
arranging the data necessary for inference, that is
to say, the knowledge of method, is everything.   It
is, Descartes adds, to his method and not to any
surpassing genius that his own discoveries have been
due.

Thus, then, a fair case can be made out for the supreme importance of the problem of method, as understood by Descartes.

And now we may follow him in his examination of the mathematical method. The characteristic of mathematical science is its certainty, and its certainty consists in this, that it starts with truths that are so simple and so self-evident that they cannot be doubted by the mind, and that nothing else is accepted as true, until it has been shown to follow necessarily from these ultimate self-evident truths. The fault of all previous philosophers is that they have neglected this method, and instead of getting back to the ultimate simple truths, upon which all others depend, have attempted the more complex problems before they have solved the simpler; have approached physical problems before they have mastered mathematics; philosophical problems before they have analysed the conceptions of which they make use.

Even Bacon reveals an ignorance of the true method, when he makes his successful attack upon the unfruitful conceptions of a false metaphysic the ground for a glorification of sense. Knowledge cannot rest upon a foundation of ignorance; and as

the sensible is the least amenable to the demands
of thought for conceptual clearness, it must remain
outside the sphere of science, till by an insight
derived from other sources its obscure complexity
has been analysed.   From experience we certainly
learn that fire melts wax and hardens clay, that the
magnet attracts iron, and innumerable other phenomena.   Since these, however, are not ultimate
'laws' of nature, but only generalised statements of
highly complex matters of fact, the whole work of
science proper still remains to be done.   Whereas the
senses reveal to us a world full of unbridgeable
qualitative differences, thought reveals the deeper
fact, that one single phenomenon, infinitely diversified,
motion in space, alone takes place.   Before we can
explain any physical phenomena, even the simplest,
we must therefore discover the laws of motion; and
when we have discovered them, we are able to deduce
the various sensible appearances from them, and to
demonstrate their necessity.   Not complex brute facts,
empirically verified, but the necessary truths involved
in our simplest conceptions, constitute the medium
of science.

Yet Descartes' method though deductive is not
syllogistic.   It is in intuition, not in the syllogism,

that our knowledge develops. If $a = b$, and $b = c$, then $a = c$. In symbolic reasoning the 'if' comes in, but when definite quantities are set in the place of the symbols, it falls away, and the truth of each is intuitively perceived. Constructing a whole out of our data, we then intuitively perceive a new relation within it.

Such a view of reasoning is very different from the scholastic theory that all knowledge is gained through the syllogism. Take the syllogism: All things equal to the same thing are equal to one another. a and c are things equal to the same thing (b), therefore a and c are equal to one another. This syllogism states the whole of the conditions upon which the truth of the conclusion rests. There is the material condition expressed in the minor, that a and c are both equal to the same third thing b: that, it will be noted, is the whole of the inference. To know the minor is practically to know the whole matter, and how that is done the syllogism makes no attempt to explain: only, once we know all we need to know, the syllogism will show what it presupposes.[1]

---

[1] "Logicians cannot form any syllogism to yield the true conclusion, if they do not already have the matter, that is to say if they do not already know the truth which they deduce by

Secondly, there is the formal condition expressed in the major, namely that it be necessary always and universally that whatsoever things are equal to a third be equal to one another. This major expresses the postulate that the laws of thought according to which we reason hold absolutely and universally, for ourselves at all times and also for all other men. The truth of the conclusion involves the truth of that postulate, and only on the assumption of its truth are we justified in asserting the conclusion. The function, therefore, of the syllogism is neither to state the reasoning process whereby we attain to a knowledge of the conclusion, nor to prove it, but solely to unfold all its implications.[1]

this means. Whence it follows that this form yields them nothing new, and that the common logic is therefore entirely useless to those who wish to discover truth, and can only be occasionally of use for expounding to others truths already known, and should therefore be transferred from philosophy to rhetoric." *Reg.* x. (xi. p. 256).

[1] Descartes' opposition to the syllogism may, in one way, be taken as following from his rejection of authority and insistence on personal verification of all truth. In using the syllogism the mind is taught *not* itself to *see* truth but to *believe* it on the authority of the syllogistic rules. The syllogism is so conclusive, logicians assert, from its mere form, that reason, while remaining itself idle, can by virtue of this form, without needing to examine the evidence offered for the conclusion, accept it as proved. To this Descartes replies, that not only does the truth

Since particular truths are known by the same process by which we apprehend the axioms, namely by intuition, and possess therefore the same intrinsic underived validity,[1] they do not require to be deduced from the universal axioms. That two plus two and three plus one are both equal to four, and therefore both equal to one another, are truths as certain as the axiom that things equal to the same thing are equal to one another; and as a matter of fact we must intuitively perceive the certainty of such particular truths before we can possibly comprehend the truth of the universal principle. And if knowledge does not consist in deduction from axioms or general principles, still less does it consist in deduction from definitions. The intuitions with which we

often escape these forms, but also that, as experience shows, by them sophistries, which would never deceive anyone who makes use only of the natural reason, entrap the sophists themselves. "And that is why, fearing above all else that our reason should remain idle while we are examining any truth, we reject those forms as contrary to our end, and prefer rather to seek all the possible means of keeping our minds attentive." *Reg.* x. (xi. pp. 255-6).

[1] Here we are stating Descartes' attitude more explicitly than he himself does, for as regards the function of the axioms he is not very clear. Cf. below, p. 37, note 2.

start must be simple and self-evident, and would therefore only be obscured by logical definitions.[1]

Though Descartes adds to intuition deduction, he does not mean by the latter anything really distinct from intuition.[2] We must, he admits, distinguish between the self-evident truths and those others whose certainty can only be discovered by deduction from them. The process, however, by which they are verified is in both cases the same. Deduction is but a series of intuitions, whereby terms not directly related are discovered to be related through their relations to intermediaries. Thus by a simple intuition the mind may apprehend that $a = b$, and by another intuition that $b = c$, and by a third that $c = d$, but in order to perceive that $a = d$ the mind has to run back and forward quickly along the whole series, and thereby gathering them together as the content of a single more complex intuition render the relation of a to d visible. The detection of that relation involves a positive increase in our knowledge, and therefore involves that intuitive process wherein alone knowledge can develop.

---

[1] *Reg.* XII. (XI. pp. 279-80). Cf. *Principles*, I. 10.
[2] *Reg.* III. (XI. pp. 213-4).

When the series is too long thus to be gathered
into a single fruitful intuition, the memory of the
evidence previously verified in intuition has to be
relied upon.

Deduction, then, is not the source of a special
kind of knowledge, but simply the process by
which intuition extends itself so as to take in the
complex that at first appears to lie outside its
sphere. Thereby intuition shows itself to be not
an isolated particular act, not an instantaneous
photograph that once taken can develop no further,
but a growing capacity of the mind for truth,
each new truth serving as an instrument for the
discovery of others. When the light of intuition
has spread from the simple truths over into the
complex, enlightening all that is obscure in them,
then, and only then, is science attained. Since
it is by one and the same act of mind that
every truth once reached is recognised, no part of
knowledge is to be regarded as more obscure than
any other.[1]

The word 'intuition' by keeping bad company,
by mixing with the self-styled 'intuitional moralists,'
has got a bad name. When we speak of intuition

[1] *Reg.* IX. XII. (XI. pp. 250, 281-2).

nowadays, we think of something unusual, of some
special faculty in the individual, and that is just
the very opposite of what Descartes means by it.
Our intuitions are not an aristocracy with a pedi-
gree other than the mass of the knowledge that
is supposed to come to us in an ordinary and
common way.   For Descartes intuition is the source
of _all_ our knowledge. Being the name which he
gives to the birth of truth in the soul, though it
is for us a word and little more, it describes a
very real fact.   Certainly, as the intuitionalists
assert, it is miraculous and a mystery, but only
in that sense of the miraculous according to which
mystery is a universal element in things.   The
mystery of intuition lies in its being one case of
growth, and therefore in its involving like all
growth the miracle of creation.   Intuition is not
a fitting together of premisses, but a dialectic.
Given certain data, they produce out of themselves
a further truth; it is a natural process, and that
is _why_ it is impossible to make a false inference.
All that the conscious mind can do, says Descartes,[1]

---

[1] _Reg._ xiv. (xi. p. 295). Cf. _Reg._ iv. (xi. pp. 216-7). ("The
science of method) cannot teach us how these operations (of
intuition and deduction) are performed, for they are the

is to prepare the conditions for its appearance.
Since to determine the nature of intuition is really
to determine the nature of consciousness or mind,
we must look for a further treatment of it to
Descartes' metaphysics.

From this new theory of reasoning Descartes
gains his answer to the double question of the
method and limits of knowledge. The limits lie,
on the one side, in the simple truths than which
nothing can be conceived more ultimate, and which
are so completely and certainly known, that no
more perfect knowledge can be desired. Descartes
calls them '*innate ideas*' and also '*simple natures.*'
They are the primary seeds of reason implanted in
us by God, and manifest their divine right by the
clearness and distinctness with which they present
themselves to the mind. The limits, in the opposite
direction, lie first in the possible fruitfulness of
the ' simple natures,' and *that*, if we may judge

simplest and most primary ; so that if our intelligence could
not previously perform them, it would not comprehend any of
the rules of method, however easy they might be." ' Intuition,'
that is to say, is the term which Descartes thinks most fitted to
describe the fact, not a theory or explanation of it, and if we
nowadays think good to reject the term, that is no refutation
of Descartes' account of reasoning. The fact remains whatever
be our theory about it.

from the proved fruitfulness of the conceptions of number, extension, figure, and motion, is inexhaustible;[1] and secondly, in the adequacy of these 'simple natures' to the comprehension of the real. We can know nothing save through the few ultimate conceptions with which our consciousness is endowed, and hence only if they express the whole nature of the real, can the real be completely known by us. Descartes' final answer to that last problem we shall learn in the next chapter.

As to the method, the secret lies in the order and disposition of our inquiries, so that we do not attempt any problem until we have the data requisite, that is, the simple intuitions in the light of which all obscurities of themselves vanish. Let us once get 'the simple natures' into our hands, and we are the masters : they are the springs of knowledge, and from them we have only to follow down the widening river of truth.

Everything, then, depends on discovery of the 'simple natures.' What are they ? The answer given

---

[1] Cf. Malebranche, *Entretiens sur la Métaphysique*, III. p. 45. "This idea (of extension) is so luminous, that geometricians and good physicists form themselves in contemplating it ; and it is so fruitful in truths, that all minds together can never exhaust it."

by Descartes in the *Regulae* agrees with the answer which he gave later in the *Principles*. [1] All things compound fall into three distinct series —material things, facts of mind, and qualities common to both. Analysing out from material things the ultimate conceptions, upon which knowledge of them depends, they are the notions of " figure, extension, motion, etc." In the mental we have as ultimate notions—" knowledge, doubt, ignorance, volition, and the like." Common to both mind and matter are " existence, duration, unity, and others similar." [2] Since these conceptions are ' simple natures,' we cannot know them at all without knowing them completely. " Otherwise we could not call them simple ; each one would be a compound of that which we know in it with that in it of which we believe ourselves ignorant." [3]

So far all is plain, but immediately we inquire how

[1] *Reg.* XII. (XI. p. 269 ff.).

[2] Descartes here adds (cf. also the *Principles*, I. 13) that to that third class belong "those common notions that are, as it were, bonds for uniting together the different simple natures, *and on the evidence of which rests every conclusion* : for example this proposition : Two things equal to a third are equal to one another." That, however, must be regarded as but a lapse back into the scholastic theory of reasoning, which he attacks.

[3] *Reg.* XII. (XI. pp. 272-3).

from these 'simple natures' the rest of knowledge is
to be developed, difficulties multiply. From any one
taken separately nothing further can be derived. The
conception of space may be contemplated in perpetuity
without anything being thereby discovered. It is, so
far, in all truth 'simple.' If, again, we compare them
together, we find indeed that figure necessarily involves
space, and that motion necessarily involves both space
and time, but other necessary relations than these
there are none. Descartes would doubtless reply to
that difficulty, that the other simple natures included
above in his '*etcetera*' must be brought in, so that
taking the angle, the line, and the number three,
along with figure and extension, we may construct
the complex figure, triangle,[1] and thereupon, by comparison of the elements making up its complexity,
discover the various properties necessarily holding
between them.

If, however, we examine these different simple natures,
we find that they have a characteristic in common,
namely, that they are one and all *abstract* conceptions,
and 'simple' only so long as they remain abstract. The
conception of space is certainly simple in the sense of

[1] *Reg.* XII. (XI. p. 275), " the nature of the triangle is composed of all these natures."

being incapable of resolution into more ultimate conceptions ; but in no other sense is it simple, for its object is not only complex, but as a concrete reality is inexhaustible in its possible modifications, forming the inexhaustible subject-matter of the science of geometry. The conception of figure is not even simple as an abstraction, since it involves the conception of space ; and it likewise owes its whole meaning to the particular and complex figures from which it is derived. Descartes, in fact, is committing the fundamental error of taking the general conceptions, through which we define and articulate the real, as being themselves in abstraction from the real the subject-matter of science. Thereby seeking to eliminate the concrete particularity of sense-perception, and so to make science purely conceptual, he falls back into the rationalistic view of knowledge, which he criticises so excellently in his attack on the syllogism.' It is as impossible to discover anything new from these ' simple natures,' as from axioms and definitions.

Here, as elsewhere, we have to distinguish between Descartes' attitude in science, and his attitude in metaphysics. So long as he is treating concrete problems, he does not go far astray. Since the ' simple natures ', are never experienced in their purity, they can only be reached by a process of analysis that starts from the concretely real. And for this analytic process Descartes is careful to lay down rules, wherein he emphasises the importance of observing and enumerating the various conditions involved in the particular phenomena examined. In these rules there is never any suggestion of an opposition between perception and conception, sense-experience being not only regarded as the source, but also as the sole source of data. In metaphysics, on the contrary, his attitude is wholly different; for there the Descartes that declared his laboratory to be his library, and praised the empirical observational method of Bacon as a valuable preparation for his own deeper one, denounces sense as alien to thought, and asserts pure conceptions to be the only legitimate organa of science.[1] And though in his metaphysics, just as in treating of physical problems, he starts from concrete experience, and seeks by means of a universal doubt to analyse out its ultimate indubitable elements, he, in the process, omits the concrete detail, and is left only with a few empty conceptions, from which he has, in accordance with his stated method, to make a pre-

[1] Cf. below, Appendix *B* to chap. III. pp. 124-6.

tence of reconstructing experience. Sense-images, he says, are of use to fix conceptions before the mind. He had perforce to admit so much, since he could not deny that in actual fact some use is made of sense-perception in mathematics and in physics. But the conceptions are, he holds, not derived from the perceptions, and in distinction from them form the subject-matter of all science.

Hence, throughout his metaphysics, Descartes speaks as if the mind could from the conceptions of extension, figure, and motion, directly develop all the particularity and variety of the real. We have only, he seems to say, attentively to contemplate them, as a magician might gaze into a crystal sphere, and they will unfold from the bosom of their transparency the whole series of properties and modifications of which they are capable. Such spontaneous generation from simple conceptions of particular modifications he not only regards as possible to them, but also declares to be their peculiar characteristic. By that strange inner power of growth, the conceptions show that they have not been framed by us; since, had the finite mind constructed them, it must have known from the start

their whole content.[1]   Inevitably, however, to make
such a view at all conceivable, he has surreptitiously
to introduce into the barren conceptions the variety
revealed in sense.   He takes, for instance, the conceptions of the different geometrical figures as given,
and has then to regard only their special properties
as conceptually generated from them.   And that
change in point of view is marked by his speaking
of the innate ideas as innumerable, citing as an
instance the notion ' triangle': " What I here find
of most importance is, that I discover in my mind
innumerable   ideas   of   certain   objects . . . which
are not framed by me, though it may be in my
power to think, or not to think them, but possess
true and immutable natures of their own.   As, for
example, when I imagine a triangle . . . "   That
idea, he proceeds to argue, though it cannot have
come into the mind through sense, can just as little
have been framed by the mind itself, for it is not
" in   any   degree   dependent   on   my   thought,   as
appears from the circumstance, that diverse properties of the triangle can be demonstrated, viz.,
that its three angles are equal to two right, that
its greatest side is subtended by its greatest angle,

[1] Cf. below, chap. III. pp. 108-10.

and the like, which, whether I will or not, I now clearly discern to belong to it, although before I did not at all think of them, when, for the first time, I imagined a triangle, and which accordingly cannot be said to have been invented by me." [1]

Now when the objects, by contemplation of which the mind acquires new knowledge, are thus regarded as conceptions, and opposed to perceptions, the view is utterly to be rejected. It is a Platonic mysticism, and not a sane rationalism. Naturally enough it led to the false rationalism of Spinoza and Leibniz, both of whom believe in the generative power of deductive reasoning, Spinoza pretending to develop the whole order of nature and of man from the single conception of divine substance, and Leibniz insisting that every necessary truth is analytic.

The radical error of Descartes shows itself plainly in his speaking of space and time as conceptual units by the combination and comparison of which with others knowledge may develop. Space is never in geometry one of the elements compared, but is that which renders possible the organisation of given data into wholes wherein new relations can be discovered. Also it is no conception, but a concrete

[1] *Meditations V.* (I. p. 310). Veitch's trans. p. 144.

reality revealed in perception, its continuity and infinite complexity being the inexhaustible source of geometrical variety. Thus if we are told that a is to the right of b, and b to the right of c, and we infer that therefore a is to the right of c, the mind does not, and cannot, derive that conclusion from the contemplation, be it ever so prolonged, of the two given separate facts, but only from the construction of a spatial whole which includes them, and determines them to have other relations besides those given. It is because the spatial whole is not an abstract conception,[1] but a concrete reality that if not perceived must be at least imaged, that it can thus progressively reveal itself to the attentive mind in new determinations. Similarly in the conception of a triangle, even though we regard it as a complex of simpler conceptions, nothing can be discovered save what has been conceived from the start. It must, in order to yield new knowledge, be con-

[1] A conception has just so much content and no more, and when clearly conceived is known completely. There cannot, to borrow a metaphor, exist in it unknown truths like opaque particles in water, that by finally dissolving may become transparent to the mind, and so reveal new relations in the old ideas. Not from a conception, which is always a completed content *in* mind, but only from a reality that in perception progressively reveals itself *to* the mind, can new knowledge arise.

structed in space, and it is because as so constructed it is capable of infinite variation, the elements composing it being so organically connected that the least variation in any one necessitates corresponding variations in all the others, that it is, as Descartes says, one of the ' seeds ' of knowledge.[1]

Descartes' method may appear to be at least an adequate account of reasoning in arithmetic and algebra, since in these sciences units conceptually fixed are by combination and recombination made to

[1] In the *Regulae* Descartes insists most emphatically on the importance of constructing our conceptions. " If the intelligence seeks to examine anything that can be related to body, it should form for itself in the imagination the most distinct idea possible. To attain that end more easily, it should set before the external senses the object that the idea represents." *Reg.* XII. (XI. p. 268). Cf. *Reg.* XIV. Also, Descartes does not in the *Regulae* separate imagination and conception as absolutely as he does later in the *Meditations.* (Compare his statements in *Reg.* XII. with his corresponding statements in *Medit.* v.) Still, spite of his being the creator of co-ordinate geometry, wherein algebra and geometry, conception and imagination, are made to co-operate, already in these *Regulae*, even while thus emphasising the importance of imagination, he speaks of the concrete images, not as indispensable sources of data, but only as external aids for fixing and rendering definite pure conceptions. For a different interpretation of Descartes' views as to the relation between imagination and understanding, cf. Natorp, *Descartes' Erkenntnisstheorie* (Marburg, 1882). Our view is supported by M. Pierre Boutroux in his pamphlet, *L'Imagination et les Mathématiques selon Descartes* (Paris, 1900).

reveal new truths. But really, as Kant was the first to point out, just as little in arithmetic and in algebra as in geometry can the combinations be derived from the isolated units. These sciences depend on the continuous nature of time, in and through which alone units are capable of combination. And it is, again, because time is a perception, not a conception, that it can render possible the discovery of ever new relations between the units in it.

We come, therefore, to the general conclusion that if the ' simple natures ' are conceptions no new knowledge can be derived from them ; and that if they are isolated units they cannot be combined. Media are necessary, and, when granted, render all talk about ' simple natures,' as so many units, impossible. Whether outside the two concrete connecting media, space and time, intuition of necessary relations is possible, and if so, what are the media that render it possible, are questions that Descartes did not see deep enough to think of raising. How very far astray his belief in the conceptual nature of science led him, we shall see in his metaphysics.

Yet while we assert Descartes' theory of method to be thus defective and incomplete, we must recognise the historical importance of his insistence on the

necessity for clearness and certainty in physics and
metaphysics as in mathematics, and of his consequent
demand that all complex conceptions be capable of
analysis into elements that are transparent to the
mind. There was only one other thinker in his day
inspired by such an intellectual ideal, and that was
Galileo, who by his pursuit of it in the physical
sphere created the science of mechanics. If, says
Descartes,[1] magnetism is a qualitatively distinct
force, and not merely the resultant of a complex of
mechanical conditions, we are forever debarred from
knowing it;[2] and we *are* debarred from knowing
all that which is not explicable in terms of the few
ultimate conceptions with which consciousness is
endowed. What these ultimate conceptions are, and
how far they render knowledge possible, it is the
work of his metaphysics to show.

[1] *Reg.* xiv. (xi. pp. 294-5). Cf. *Reg.* xii. p. 281.
[2] To know it "we should require either new senses or a
divine mind." *Loc. cit.*

CHAPTER III.

THE METAPHYSICS OF DESCARTES.

THE instrument which Descartes uses for analysing out from experience the ultimate conceptions upon which it rests, is doubt, and on applying it he finds that there is only one truth which is altogether indubitable, the *cogito ergo sum* of Augustine. 'If nothing of all that I doubt exists, yet still my doubt remains. If all that I perceive is illusory, yet none the less my perception remains. If all that I imagine be purely fictitious, it is yet true that I imagine. And all these, doubt, perception, imagining, are forms of consciousness, modes of thought. Consciousness, therefore, or thinking, is that which is beyond the possibility of all doubt.' We know our ideas face to face, and they are as we perceive them to be. It is only when we go out beyond them, and assert the existence of something outside corresponding to them, that we can fall into error. The inner self-transparency of thought which sees itself, and can see nothing save as reflected in itself, is the sole indubitable certainty, the one form of existence directly known to us.

Now the *cogito ergo sum*, considered as the primary certainty in our knowledge, can be regarded in two ways, either as a necessary truth of reason, and then it must be universally expressed, wherever there is consciousness there is existence, or as conveying our certainty as to a particular contingent fact, namely, that I in being conscious exist at this particular moment. Interpreting Descartes in accordance with his treatment of the intuitive truths of mathematics, we find that the two aspects of the *cogito* are inseparable. A universal mathematical truth, we have seen, is always apprehended in and through the particular, the particular case being apprehended as an illustration of the universal, and the universal truth as involved in the particular. So also is it in the *cogito* which Descartes uses in both interpretations.

When used, however, to prove existence, the ' I ' is illegitimately brought in. The present consciousness does not afford us any indubitable certainty of our having existed in the past or of continuing to exist in the future, and yet such implications of continuity of existence the use of the ' I ' certainly

involves.   Still less does immediate consciousness
prove the existence of the self as a simple indivisble
substance.   Descartes in so arguing really interprets
his 'ultimate' principle in accordance with an
assumed principle yet more ultimate, in logical though
not in temporal order, the principle namely, which he
explicitly states in his *Principles*[1], as a truth
manifest by the natural light of reason, "that to
nothing no affections or qualities belong." Thought
he, without proof, assumes to be a quality, and
therefore, in accordance with that principle, to imply
a substance or self.[2]

Descartes, however, is also interested to derive
from the *cogito* a universal criterion of truth, and in so
doing interprets it in the universal way, as a necessary
truth of reason, showing the inseparability of the idea
of consciousness from the idea of existence.   Such
inseparability in thought, if in this case a sufficient
proof of inseparability in fact, must be so in all cases.
And his universal criterion of truth and reality therefore is, that all that in thought is clearly and

[1] I. II. (III. p. 69).

[2] That, too, is how Malebranche and Regis interpret
Descartes' argument.   Cf. Malebranche, *Entretiens sur la Meta-
physique*, I. p. 5 ; and Regis, *Cours Entier de Philosophie* : *la
Métaphysique*, liv. I. pt. I. chap. XI. p. 96.

distinctly conceived to be necessarily connected must be likewise inseparable in existence.   It will be noted that the universal truth (the idea of existence is inseparable from the idea of consciousness) is not proved by the particular intuitive judgment, *cogito ergo sum*, but only illustrated in it, and still less, therefore, can the *cogito* prove the yet more universal criterion of truth.

Now we must urge against the exaggerated importance which Descartes attaches to the *cogito ergo sum*, that we never need to prove existence, since we can never get away from it, but only to define it. When Descartes shows that consciousness involves existence he proves, only too truly, what can never be doubted, since, if existence is thus taken quite vaguely, it is certain that all the objects we perceive even in dreams exist.   When, on the other hand, he pretends to have proved by the *cogito* the existence of the self as a spiritual substance he asserts what it can never prove.   As proving existence, therefore, the *cogito* is superfluous, and for defining it, it is useless.

Descartes, indeed, by adopting the doctrine of representative perception[1] as a necessary consequence

[1] Descartes' argument in the first *Meditation* most evidently rests on an interpretation of knowledge in the light of that

of the dualism from which he starts, made inevitable
for himself the view that only in consciousness can
we come into direct contact with reality. And
further, since throughout his metaphysics he almost
invariably assumes that ideas are distinct from the
mind, and that over against them stands a self that
contemplates them, the existence of ideas is for him
sufficient proof of the self's existence. In the
doctrine of representative perception is thus contained all that is of importance in the *cogito.* We
can know only ideas, but as we know them face to
face we cannot doubt either their existence or the
existence of the self whose thought they terminate.[1]

Since the criterion of truth is not proved by
the *cogito ergo sum,* but only illustrated in it, it still

doctrine. What is implied by Descartes is explicitly stated
by Malebranche, viz., that the doctrine of representative perception is a self-evident truth. Cf. *Recherche*, III. pt. II. chap. I.
p. 377, which has already been quoted below in note to page 5.
Arnauld was the only member of the Cartesian school who
thought of questioning this doctrine. Cf. Appendix A to this
chapter, p. 115.

[1] Leibniz, in differing from Descartes, is really only making
Descartes' own position more explicit. Cf. *Nouveaux Essais*, liv.
vi., chap. II. sec. I. (Gerhardt, v. p. 347): " It is not only immediately clear to me that *I think*, but it is just as clear to
me that I have *different thoughts*. . . . Thus the Cartesian
principle is sound, but is not the only one of its kind."

remains to be asked why, and with what right, we trust to that criterion. Why must that which is true for us and in the mind, be true for all others and outside the mind ? Descartes replies by unfolding the implications that underlie the acceptance of the *cogito ergo sum* as a necessary truth. Though we cannot doubt of any intuitive truth when it is present to the mind,[1] we can yet when we look back in memory on a conclusion that has been established by a chain of such intuitive truths, distrust the validity of that conclusion, so long as we do not repeat in thought and so verify in fact the necessity of belief in each of the intuitions that compel its acceptance. And, further, the doubt, when it is thus kept detached from special simple intuitions, can become perfectly universal : all our ideas, and therefore all the truths that we perceive to be necessarily involved in them, may one and all be false, being implanted in us by some evil genius. As the possibility that two and two should *not* make four, is only conceivable on the assumption that the faculty of knowing is in its essential nature deceptive, and that therefore all knowledge is an illusion, this general doubt is the only form of doubt applicable to our simplest intui-

[1] *Principles*, i. 13 (iii. pp. 71-2).

tions. Clear and distinct conception is a valid criterion in all cases or in none. Between rationalism and scepticism there is no alternative.

Descartes, however, refuses to recognise this fact, and seeks to compound with reason in an impossible compromise. He will trust reason just so far as he sees to be necessary to establish the existence of God, and will then throw on God the responsibility of an unlimited trust. To avoid following him into the sophistries that such a view necessitates, we shall interpret his line of thought according to the higher truth that forces him to seek to conceal the *petitio principii* that such argument involves.[1] The acceptance of any truth, the *cogito ergo sum* or any other, involves the acceptance of the universal criterion of truth, and therefore the acceptance of all that thought, in accordance with that criterion, shows to be necessary. Everything or nothing is what reason demands, and since to act is a necessity, the alternative to be chosen is decided for us.

In his proofs of the existence of God Descartes'

---

[1] The *petitio principii* lies in his using principles, which he holds to be truths evident by the natural light of reason, to prove God's existence, and then guaranteeing the validity of reason by the veracity of God.

scholasticism comes to a height. Usually he conceives God as a creator; and when he dispenses with that obscure conception, it is only to fall back upon the equally obscure notion of substance. As it is hopeless to attempt to disentangle the diverse lines of thought involved in his arguments save by means of the clarifying analyses which Locke and Hume made of these fundamental conceptions, we shall in the meantime consider his arguments only so far as is necessary to maintain the continuity of his thinking.

Starting with the assumption that creation is not only intelligible, but also the sole conceivable ultimate explanation of origin, Descartes lays down as principles " evident by the natural light of reason," that nothing cannot be the cause of anything, and that the more perfect cannot arise from the less perfect, so as to be thereby produced as by its efficient and total cause, and that, therefore, all that is contained in an idea, or as it were in a picture, must exist in its first and chief cause not only in idea but also in fact.[1] We find in the mind the idea of God as an absolutely perfect being, and as we do not in any way find in ourselves the perfections contained in that idea, we must conclude that they exist in

[1] *Principles*, I. 17 (III. p. 74).

some nature different from ours, that is, in God, who must, therefore, be inferred to exist in order to cause the idea in us.

And, again, starting from this other principle 'in the highest degree self-evident,' that it is more difficult to create substance than any of the attributes of substance,[1] it must be inferred that, if we had made ourselves, we should have made ourselves perfect in all our properties. But as we have the knowledge of many perfections which we do not possess, we must have drawn our origin from no other being than from him who possesses in himself all those perfections. Again, therefore, God must exist.

And, thirdly, to meet the objection that the idea of an infinite all-perfect being may be derived from experience by a combination, and ideal completion, of the perfections we meet there, Descartes replies that it cannot be so, since the idea of the infinite is involved in all consciousness of the finite as its prior condition. "For how," he asks, "could I know

---

[1] *Principles*, I. 20 (III. pp. 76-7). Regis therefrom infers that "all substances, with the exception of God, are equally perfect in themselves" (*Cours Entier: la Métaphysique*, liv. I. pt. I. chap. XII. p. 100).

that I doubt, desire, or that something is wanting to me, and that I am not wholly perfect, if I possessed no idea of a being more perfect than myself, by comparison of which I know the deficiencies of my nature ? " [1]   The idea of God is, therefore, the primary fact in our consciousness, and makes possible the consciousness of the self as a doubting finite being.   It is not merely as clear and distinct as the consciousness of the self's existence, but clearer, since only through its mediation is such consciousness possible.   And with an over-emphasis that is highly significant, Descartes concludes that there can be no idea " more true or less open to the suspicion of falsity." [2]

That last argument leads up to, and indeed involves, the ontological argument.   If we take any geometrical conception, say that of a triangle, from the mere conception we can deduce with absolute certainty that the sum of its angles is equal to two right angles.   So, too, from the mere idea or conception of God we can deduce certain properties as necessarily belonging to Him, and one of these properties is His existence.   It is as impossible to conceive a Being absolutely perfect to whom the

[1] *Medit.* iii. (i. p. 281).   Veitch's trans. p. 126.   [2] *Loc. cit.*

perfection of actual real existence is yet awanting, as to conceive a circle while denying that its radii are all equal. Consequently it is as certain that God, who is this perfect Being, is or exists, as any demonstration of geometry can be.

Now, the ontological argument by itself merely proves a necessity of thought, the necessity of thinking God as existing, if we think Him at all. The idea of God may be purely fictitious, and hence the necessity it lays upon the mind of adding the further idea of necessary existence may be a fictitious necessity. There are certain laws of thought that we cannot escape even in the most imaginary of ideal worlds, but that in these ideal worlds we are still subject to the tyranny of some necessity or other does not make them to be real. It must be proved that the idea of a perfect being is no such arbitrary idea, but an idea which the mind has not fabricated for itself, and which it must think if it is to think at all. The ontological argument, therefore, rests on and presupposes the preceding arguments whereby that has been proved.[1]

[1] The connection should be noted of the ontological argument in the fifth *Meditation* with the proof that immediately precedes it, that conceptions are all objective and given to the

And now that Descartes has established the existence of God, he is able to overthrow all the sceptical
doubts, through which alone he was forced to reject
the truths of reason as possibly false.   This result
he expresses in a very crude form, saying that one
of the qualities belonging to God's perfection is
veracity, and that, therefore, He cannot will to
deceive us.   What Descartes means thereby, is that
God is the all-comprehensive absolute reality, in

mind, not framed by its own finite powers.   Cf. below, pp.
108-10 in this chapter.

It is not true, we have seen in the preceding chapter, that
from the mere abstract conception of a triangle, as a space
enclosed by three straight lines, the other properties of the
triangle are discoverable, but only from the construction of it
in space.   It is because it is a perception that it can reveal new
properties, not originally thought in it, to the mind.   The conception of God, however, is a pure conception, and therefore if
it involves existence, such necessary existence must have been
explicitly conceived in it from the start.   The bearing of this
will appear in the chapter on Locke (p. 199).   We shall see how
the conception of God, regarded as the Unconditioned, is just
the conception of absolute existence and nothing more, the
quality of perfection being illegitimately used as a metaphorical
synonym for absoluteness.   Only because the idea of God can
be interpreted in these two ways, either as denoting a personal
moral agent, or as signifying the absolute reality in whom we
and all other beings are contained, can Descartes, while offering
proofs of God's existence, still claim that no idea is "more true
or less open to the suspicion of falsity."

whom we as well as all other beings are contained, and that in Him truth and existence are one. The necessity which constrains us to think in a certain way is likewise a necessity which governs real existence. The nature of things is rational, and hence rationalism is the true philosophy. All that we clearly and distinctly conceive to be true, we may safely accept as true.

Descartes, however, not only interprets that criterion as meaning that what is inseparable in thought is inseparable in the real, but also adds the negative interpretation that in the case of ideas between which the mind can perceive no connection, the existences corresponding to them must also be unconnected. What misled him was the scholastic doctrine that each substance has an essence peculiar to itself, which constitutes it what it is, and is inseparable from its existence, and that a sharp line can be drawn between this essence and all else. Though this teaching results in a conceptual atomism, which is the direct opposite of the modern scientific point of view, and of Descartes' own point of view in his physics, according to which to know any material thing we must relate it to other things and ultimately to the whole universe, it was estab-

lished by an argument whose force, trifling as it now
appears, Descartes was unable to withstand. A
thing must either exist or not exist : there is no
third alternative. Further, it must exist altogether,
with the whole of its essence, or not at all. And
so, too, the scholastic mind argued, if it be clearly
and distinctly conceived, it must be conceived altogether, through the whole of its essence, since what
we mean by essence is that without which a thing
can neither be nor be conceived. *Substance, essence,
and conception are all identical, and hence what is not
essential to the conception of the thing is not essential
to its existence.*[1] Applying his criterion, interpreted
in this negative way, Descartes argues, that since

---

[1] Cf. Regis, *Cours Entier : la Métaph.* liv. I. pt. I. chap. II.
axiom 4 : " that the essences of things are indivisible, and that
we can neither add to them nor diminish them without destroying them." Cf. Malebranche, *Recherche,* liv. III. pt. II. chap.
VIII. p. 422 : " Philosophers sufficiently agree that we ought to
regard as the essence of a thing that which is recognised as
primary in it, that which is inseparable from it, and on which
depend all the properties that belong to it." Malebranche adds
in a note that " if we accept this definition of the word *essence,*
all the rest is absolutely demonstrated." Malebranche also
explicitly states on p. 424, as an indubitable truth, the further
principle, assumed both by himself and by Descartes, viz., that
everything must either be a substance or the modification of a
substance.

pure thought alone is inseparable from the mind, it by itself constitutes its whole essence ; and similarly that extension constitutes the whole essence of matter; and that the two, mind and matter, are wholly independent of one another. Sensations and feelings must have been introduced into mind, and motion into matter, from the outside.[1]

One consequence of this identification of substance and conception is that there can be no mean for Descartes between complete knowledge and absolute ignorance.[2] The continual reference to God for explanation of finite phenomena is no admission, as so many of his commentators assume, of ignorance of the true explanation, but is always based on the certain and absolute knowledge that they are due neither to mind

---

[1] A detailed account of Descartes' argument is given in Appendix B at the end of this chapter, p. 117. Those readers who are not acquainted with Descartes' theory of perception, or with his account of the relation between sense and understanding, are requested to read this appendix before proceeding, as a knowledge of Descartes' views on these points is presupposed in what follows.

[2] Consistently that is, for it need hardly be pointed out how inconsistent is his assertion of partial knowledge of God, since he tells us that the idea of God is the clearest and most distinct we possess. Another difficulty for Descartes is how, if extension is completely known, new knowledge can continuously be acquired of its ' modes.'   Cf. below, p. 68, note 2.

nor to matter (these being known completely), and that
therefore, so far as they have any reality, they must
be wholly dependent on what is outside both. It is
by such a process of *exclusion* (a form of argument
very important in the Cartesian system), that the
phenomena are preferred to God as the only remaining
reality.   On this assumption of completed knowledge
also rests, we may repeat, Descartes' negative interpretation of the criterion of truth.   Since mind and body
are in thought completely transparent to us, each
being exhaustively known in conception, where no
necessary connection is visible between them, or
between either of them and what is conjoined with it in
experience, there can be none, and such conjunction as
is vouched for by experience must be regarded as
external and contingent.   There can, therefore, be no
rationalising of Descartes' implicit occasionalism without desertion of his whole metaphysical position.   His
metaphysics is, we shall see, the demonstration of the
impossibility either of explaining one finite fact from
another, or of deducing the finite rationally from the
infinite.[1]   There is required in order that his system,

---

[1] If it is to be rescued from such a suicidal admission, *without
desertion of the doctrine of substance* (as that which has all its
reality and relations within itself), that can only be at the

which thus comes to be not only dualistic but also atomistic, may march at all, even in an artificial galvanised manner, the conception of a third kind of reality capable of bringing about such connection as the finite substances, be they spiritual or material, cannot by themselves achieve.   That is the real ground for Descartes' inevitable assumption of God's existence, and in comparison his official arguments are of secondary importance.

Having thus gained and guaranteed the criterion of truth, Descartes applies it at once to the concrete contents of mind, and the problem, under which I shall bring all the other points I wish to raise in his metaphysics, is the problem deferred from the last chapter, as to what he determines the ultimate conceptions or innate ideas to be, under how many categories he brings them, and how on his view they are interrelated.   In solving that problem, Descartes gives

expense of the dualism.   Either the finite substances must be made absolute or they must be taken up into the absolute.   We must either with Leibniz pulverise the real into atoms (each of them conceived as a complete world in itself), or with Spinoza, identify it with the one indivisible divine substance.   The Leibnizian position is (if we can make such comparisons) the more natural to Descartes, and that to which he most tends, the mystic synthetic religious pantheism of Spinoza being wholly alien to his plastic analytic purely intellectual cast of mind.

his answer to the question as to the limits of knowledge. Since, as he has shown in his doctrine of method, the only knowledge possible to the mind is that which is deducible from the innate ideas, our knowledge will reach just so far as they do and no farther.

Taking first the conceptions involved in the comprehension of the material world, they can all be brought under the categories of matter, extension, figure, and motion. Through these the whole nature of the material half of the universe is, Descartes holds, completely known. By regarding extension as constituting the whole essence of matter,[1] Descartes destroyed the belief, almost universal in his day, that a tenuous and subtle fluid (such as air, and also fire as then conceived) approximates to the spiritual. When a gross substance is subtilised into a rare fluid, it does not, Descartes easily demonstrates, thereby become any the less material. This identification of space with matter has, however, found many opponents. Locke, for instance, takes the feeling of resistance as revealing the objective quality of solidity. To that objection Descartes replies that, since the feeling of resistance is as variable as the sensations of colour and heat, and

[1] Cf. Appendix *B* at the end of this chapter, pp. 117 ff.

equally inconceivable save as in a mind that is capable of feeling, it must be regarded as likewise subjective. Descartes further shows that by the solidity of a body we can mean nothing more than that it is extended, and so fills a certain space. Space cannot be filled twice over, and hence matter as filling space is *ipso facto* solid. Another criticism made is that (since no part of space can go outside itself to visit a neighbouring space) if matter is extension it cannot be moved. That objection, however, rests on a false interpretation of Descartes' teaching. He does not say that matter is space, but contrariwise that spatial extension is the essence of matter. Matter alone has substantial reality, space being ' by a distinction of reason ' conceived as its attribute. A particular space (definable and conceivable only as a particular set of relations holding between bodies at least relatively fixed) though inseparable from body, is not inseparable from any particular body. When water is poured from a vessel, the space vacated by the water is immediately taken by air, and hence the spatial relations holding between the sides of the vessel persist. Matter may move, though the space thus defined remains. Geulincx [1] gives a very subtle, but quite sufficient answer to the one

[1] *Metaphysica Vera* : II. Quinta Scientia.

remaining difficulty : how, if space is body, we can yet, as we continually do, speak of body as in space. Obviously body cannot be in body, since all body excludes body.   When we thus speak of bodies being in space, we mean, Geulincx replies, particular bodies. Such particular things are material but not matter : they are distinguished from matter by their motion, and therefore are in matter like the motion that constitutes them.[1]

But, while we grant that the above objections can all be met, there is still one criticism that must be made, namely, that Descartes uses the conception of substance and attribute to define the relation of space to matter, and yet nowhere analyses this category.   Just as his dogmatic use of the similarly unanalysed conception of causality, that principle 'evident by the natural light of reason,' to denote the relation (on his theory in-conceivable) of soul and body, directly gave rise to the destructive criticism of it by the occasionalists and Hume, so too the difficulties involved in this identification of extension with

---

[1] Matter, it must be borne in mind, is regarded by Descartes as homogeneous and continuous, motion being the *sole* differen-tiating factor.   To mind all the secondary qualities are due. Cf. below, note 2, p. 68.

matter, as also of pure thought with mind, impelled both Locke and Leibniz to the examination
of the conception thus employed.[1]

Figure is a modification of space, and is, therefore, correctly enough described as a *mode* of space,
though of course that is a mere description and no
adequate account of their connection.[2] Descartes,
however, also defines the relation of motion to
extension, and therefore to matter, by that same
term, and thereby commits one of his fundamental

---

[1] While Spinoza and Leibniz both retain Descartes' definition
of substance, as that which contains all its relations within
itself, the former drew the conclusion that it is only applicable
to the Divine Being, and the latter (virtually regarding the
distinction between the finite individual and God as merely one
of degree) the similar conclusion that each finite substance must
contain within its content the notion of the whole universe.
Cf. Descartes' statements in the *Principles*, I. 51 (III. pp. 94-5) on
the impossibility of applying the term substance in the same
sense at once to God and to created beings.

[2] If bare extension is the whole essence of matter, then figure
must be introduced from outside as well as motion, and as a
matter of fact is so *physically*, since the differences of figure in
matter result from motion, and depend on its continuance. And
conceptually it must be so likewise, though Descartes ignores
the difficulty by constantly speaking as if all figures were
directly deducible by pure thought from extension. Malebranche
as usual boldly faces the problem, and explains the appearance
of figures in intelligible space as due to differences arising in
sense (an exact parallel to the physical explanation of them as
arising from motion). Under the stimulus of sense we attach

errors. The great achievement of Galileo and Descartes in physical science consisted in a new theory of motion. Whereas by the Greek Atomists and by Aristotle motion was anthropomorphically conceived, as, like human activity, coming into being, exhausting itself in exercise against obstacles, and ceasing to be—the fleeting activity of a matter that is alone abiding; with Galileo and Descartes it asserts its full rights. It is, they show, in its ingenerable, indestructible nature, as different from human activity as matter is from mind. Galileo did not, however, realise the full significance of his discoveries; and it was left to Descartes to state the difficulties involved in any attempt to derive motion from matter, or to connect it in any necessary way with matter. Matter and motion, as conceived by Descartes, are quite distinct in nature

different sensations of colour to the homogeneous unfigured space, and so there arise *for us* different figures in it. Malebranche's explanation applies, however, only to the *perception* of figure. If colour be removed figure disappears too, and only bare extension remains. The pure *conception* of figure is still left unaccounted for. Descartes' whole treatment of figure and its relation to space, whether in his method or in his metaphysics, is very unsatisfactory, and that by no accident, since 'modes' of any kind are the crux of his philosophy. For Spinoza's attitude towards this problem cf. below, chapter IV. pp. 153 ff.

and in origin;[1] and *equally substantial,* since they are equally ingenerable out of nothing, and equally indestructible. Indeed, Descartes so far anticipated modern science as completely to reverse the rôles hitherto played by matter and motion. In Greek science the differences between natural phenomena are ascribed to differences in matter, either to differences between atoms or to differences between elements: in Descartes' philosophy of nature, as in modern science, they are ascribed to differences of motion. Matter becomes the mere vehicle of motion, and motion the all-important reality.

Strictly, therefore, Descartes' analysis of the real lands him not in a dualism, but in a trinity, and in a trinity one of whose elements mediates between the other two. Motion, like matter, is unconscious, but also, like mind, is unextended, immaterial, and active.[2] The fictitious dualism conceals a purely relative trinity of the three substantial realities, matter, motion, and mind.[3]

---

[1] Cf. Appendix *B* at the end of this chapter, p. 121.

[2] At least as active as he shows mind to be.

[3] There still remains, of course, a dualism, with matter and motion on the one side and mind on the other, but once motion is admitted to be equally real with matter the dualism cannot be formulated in the absolute manner of Descartes.

That, however, is only the position which Descartes takes up in his physics. In his metaphysical exposition of his physical views he inconsistently speaks of motion as a mere mode or form of matter, his sole argument for so regarding it, as a dependency of matter, being that while extension, which constitutes the essence of matter, is conceivable apart from motion, motion cannot be conceived apart from it. That argument, even granting it to be a legitimate one,[1] is disposed of by Kant when he shows that we can only conceive a line by drawing it in thought, a process which involves motion.[2] The reason of this misrepresentation of his physical theory is to be found in his scholastically interpreted criterion of truth. The ideal of knowledge, which that criterion so interpreted involves, is wholly inconsistent with explanation by efficient mechanical causes. Rational connection and physical causation form two distinct kinds of knowledge: the one yields necessary truth that justifies itself by its inevitableness for thought, the other (so Hume urges and Kant agrees), contingent for

[1] The same argument would prove motion to be a mode of time.

[2] The conceptions of time, space, and motion, Kant proves, mutually involve one another.

thought, can only be empirically ascertained.[1] As Descartes' rationalistic ideal is constructed solely in the light of the first kind of knowledge, he has, in order to maintain its universality, to explain the other away. That is what in his metaphysics he has come, at least partially, to recognise.[2]

First, he admits that thought can never establish necessity of existence. Since never in the conception of any finite thing is existence involved, we are forced in accordance with the criterion of truth to regard its existence as contingent, that is to say, as unaccountable by reason, and therefore, in Descartes' way of stating it, as due to the arbitrary will of God. But, further, not only is each finite thing contingent in its origin, so also is its continued existence, that also being inexplicable from its essence. Since each moment of time is distinct from every other,[3] the persistence of an existence

---

[1] Whatever ultimately be the connection between the principle of sufficient reason and the law of causality, cause and reason certainly cannot be straight away identified ; and yet that is what Descartes by his principles is forced to do.

[2] As we shall see in the next chapter, this consequence is recognised by Leibniz and Spinoza, both of whom identify causation with explanation. The same identification is at the root of the occasionalist denial of transient action.

[3] It may at first sight seem strange that Descartes, who

from one moment on to another demands an explanation as much as its first origin, and yet again none can be given, save only the will of God. Persistence in existence, says Descartes, is in all essentials perpetual and unceasing recreation.[1]

And if existence is thus in all its forms inexplicable, how much more so is causation! Since persistence in existence is traced to God, so consistently must everything else. If finite bodies have so little hold on reality that they require at each moment to be recreated, they cannot be capable of causing changes in one another: not having sufficient

emphasises the continuity of space, should yet regard time as discrete, but the truth is that his atomistic rationalism is wholly inconsistent with the continuity of either space or time. (Cf. below, chap. iv. p. 170.) The view of time which Descartes is thus forced to advocate is also bound up with his scholastic theology; and, as it casts some light upon his metaphysics, we have considered it more at length in Appendix *C* at the end of this chapter, p. 128.

[1] *Principles*, i. 21 (iii. p. 77), Veitch's trans. p. 202: "The truth of this demonstration [that the duration alone of our life is sufficient to demonstrate the existence of God] will clearly appear, provided we consider the nature of time, or the duration of things; for this is of such a kind that its parts are not mutually dependent, and never co-existent; and, accordingly, from the fact that we now are, it does not necessarily follow that we shall be a moment afterwards, unless some cause—viz., that which first produced us—shall, as it were, continually reproduce us, that is, conserve us."

reality to persist, they cannot have sufficient force to act.[1] The most extreme occasionalism is, therefore, the outcome of Descartes' metaphysics. The continuity of existence, and therefore the continuity of time and of causal connection in time, is broken up by his atomistic doctrine of essence into a series of detached events upheld in their existence and connection by God. God must, in his continuous recreation of things, be regarded as continuously modifying them in accordance with a plan, the fixed though arbitrary[2] modes, in which He acts in the realisation of this plan, being what we mean by the laws of nature.

[1] Cf. below, Appendix C, pp. 129-31. Even though bodies could act on one another, as they do not persist, they cannot bear the effects of other things, save as these are recognised by God in their recreation.

[2] Though Descartes recognises that the laws of motion, which are the sole ultimate laws of nature, are not, like the truths of mathematics, demonstrable as being rationally necessary, he still pretends to give a ' deduction ' of them. They are, he says, necessary consequences of the unchangeableness of God's will. Malebranche, at first, in a similar way, regarded them as consequences of the law of economy (the use of the simplest means to a fixed end) which God as divinely wise obeys in all His works ; but later, under the influence of Leibniz, he admitted that even such justification of them is impossible, and that it is only "by a species of revelation such as experience supplies" that they can be determined. Cf. Malebranche's *Traité des Loix de la Communication des Mouvemens* (published 1692).

A more detailed examination of Descartes' treatment of motion will serve to confirm the above statements. Descartes really interprets motion in two ways, geometrically and dynamically, the resulting views being quite inconsistent with one another. From the geometrical point of view (which is emphasised in his metaphysics) motion is mere transference from one place to another. So regarded it is a *mode* of extension, and is even better known than figure, as is proved by its use in geometry to account for differences of figure. A further consequence is that, being a mode of the particular body moved, it cannot any more than the other modes of that body be regarded either as transferable or as indestructible. Like figure, when it ceases to be in one particular body, it must cease altogether.

Descartes could not, however, consistently hold to that geometrical view of motion, as a *mode* of matter, since it would have forced him to adopt one of two disagreeable alternatives. Either, first, motion being as untransferable as figure, he would have had to ascribe to each particular body the power of creating new motion in other bodies on impact. Or, secondly, he would have been forced to admit that body is incapable of acting on body, and that therefore God is the sole Mover.

To escape these alternatives, while still speaking of motion as a mode, he inconsistently continues to conceive it as a separate entity, distinct both from God who has created it, and from the matter in which it may exist in varying quantities. It is to all intents and purposes conceived as existing in matter like a salt dissolved in water.[1] Also, being known only through its mysteriously generated effect (motion in the geometrical sense, as change of place), it must be regarded as an unknown and incomprehensible substance, divisible like matter, but incorporeal like mind. It therefore overthrows not only Descartes' dualism, but also his claim to completed comprehension of material phenomena. " Do our senses teach us," De la Forge asks, " how motion can pass from one body to another ? Why there is transferred only a part of it, and why a body cannot communicate its motion in the same manner as a teacher communicates his knowledge, without losing any of that which he gives ? The cause of the motion

---

[1] A metaphor actually used by Rohault according to Leibniz, though we have been unable to identify the reference. Cf. Leibniz, *Nouveaux Essais*, liv. II. chap. XXIII. (Gerhardt, v. p. 208).

of bodies is not then so simple a matter as one might think."[1]

It is worthy of note that, when pressed upon this point by More,[2] Descartes has to admit the inconsistency of his views, and that the alternative which he chooses is occasionalism. More is very definite and clear in his criticisms. He insists in his letter to Descartes on the distinction between motion and the force causing motion, and adds that if motion be identified with change of place, and so be regarded as a mode, it cannot any more than figure pass from one body to another. "And finally, I am filled with amazement, when I consider that so slight and mean a thing as motion, which can be separated from its subject and pass into another body, and which besides is of so feeble and transitory a nature that it would at once perish if it were not sustained by its subject, should yet affect it so powerfully, and drive it with

[1] *Traité de l'Esprit de l'Homme* (pub. 1666), chap. XVI. pp. 242-3. It has been asserted (cf. Stein, *Archiv für Geschichte der Philosophie*, I. p. 53) that this treatise was published in 1661, but as 1666 is the date on the title-page, and as De la Forge in one of his notes (I, I, b) to the 1664 edition of Descartes' *L'Homme* himself speaks of his treatise *as about to appear*, we retain the later date.

[2] Henry More (1614-1687) was one of the Cambridge Platonists.

such force hither and thither."[1]   Descartes' reply to
the first point is, so far as it has any definiteness,
an acceptance of the extreme occasionalist position.
He admits the distinction between motion as mere
transference and motion in the sense of moving
force.   While the first is a mere mode of matter,
the second comes from God who continuously preserves the same amount of transference (*translatio*) in
matter, as He has set into it at the first moment
of Creation.   Descartes further states that the
reason why he has not emphasised this distinction
in his writings is that it is rather beyond the reach
of the vulgar, and might seem to favour the opinion
of those who believe God to be the soul of the world
and to be united to matter.

In replying to More's second objection, Descartes
makes his occasionalism still more explicit.   "You
rightly observe that motion, so far as it is a mode

[1] *Lett.* x. p. 255.   More is inclined to believe that there is
no communication of motion, and that the impact of one body
on another is only the occasion whereupon the other is determined to move, just as the mind has this or that thought
on the occasion of this or that motion in the brain.   "Motion
is in relation to body that which thought is in relation to
mind : neither the one nor the other is received into the subject,
but both have their birth from the subject in which they are
found."

of body, cannot pass from one body to another. But neither have I asserted that. Rather I believe that motion, so far as it is such a mode, is in a state of continuous change. . . . *When I have said that the amount of motion in matter remains constant, I have understood that of the force impelling its parts, which force now applies itself to some parts of body, and now to others.* You need not therefore worry yourself over the transference of rest from one body to another, since not even motion, so far as it is a mode opposed to rest, can be so transferred."[1]

Descartes, however, had no liking for the occasionalism in which he is thus entrapped by his rationalism. Not only does he still continue in his published works to speak as if bodies transmitted motion by impact, but also to assert that mind and body interact in sense-perception and in volition.[2]

---

[1] *Lett.* x. pp. 294-6.

[2] Descartes was led to believe that soul and body interact through one particular part of the brain, namely the pineal gland, first by the fact that it seemed to be the one organ in the brain which is not double, and which, therefore, is capable of combining the impressions made on the different parts of the brain, and especially the twofold impressions from the double organs of sight and hearing; and secondly, by the fact that having a central position in the brain, it is fitted

Senses

First, as to sense-perception. He had been able in his physics to reduce external objects to extension, figure, and motion, only by separating off from the objects all their other qualities and ascribing these to the mind. But later, when he had demonstrated that the whole essence of the self consists in pure thought, and that sense and imagination are quite distinct from pure thought,[1] the problem arose how these sensations can exist in mind any more than in matter. To solve the difficulty he modifies his dualism. Just as external objects acquire the secondary qualities only through being brought into relation to the mind, so too, he holds, sensations and images can only arise in the mind through its union with a material body. Corresponding to our pure conceptions there are, he dogmatically asserts, no brain processes. Conception is a purely spiritual process, and wholly independent of the body. Sense and imagination, on the other hand, are conditioned by

to control the movements of those 'animal spirits,' which in his theory correspond to the nervous currents of modern physiology. The animal spirits move the pineal gland, and thereby rouse in the mind sensations and feelings. Similarly the mind, by setting the pineal gland in motion, affects a change in the course of the animal spirits, and so brings about movement in the members of the body.

[1] See Appendix *B* at the end of this chapter, pp. 126-7.

brain-processes, and without them are not possible.[1]
This attempt, however, to explain the rise of sensations and images by the action of body on mind
wholly fails, since even in sense and imagination
mind and body must be regarded as perfectly
distinct. The states of the brain are but modes of
matter and motion, and hence entirely different from
the sensations and images which correspond to them
in the mind. There can be no metamorphosis of
the brain state into the mental state. Dead unfeeling
matter cannot hand over to the mind sensations ready
made. Nothing, Descartes says in one of his letters,
can come into the mind from outside through the
senses, whence it follows that " the ideas of pain, of
colours, sounds, and all such things must be natural
to the mind," that is, innate in it.[2] The action of
the body on the mind in perception can at most be
but the occasion or stimulus which determines the
mind to produce the sensation out of itself at this

[1] See Descartes' curious statements, by no means reconcilable
with the rest of his teaching, as to the nature of imagination,
which are quoted below in Appendix *B*, note 2 to p. 126.

[2] *Lett.* x. p. 96. Cf. *L'Homme*, iv. p. 361. Thus Descartes is
in the end forced to give up the distinction, which he draws
in the third *Meditation*, between innate and adventitious
ideas.

particular moment rather than at any other. Now that is the very admission which Descartes sought to avoid. He violates his dualism so far as to admit that body can act on mind, but with no good result, since the same problem still remains, how sensations can arise in a mind whose whole essence consists in pure thought. Sensations he can explain as due neither to mind in itself, nor to body in itself, nor to the two in union.

Secondly, with regard to the action of mind on body in volition, Descartes kept consistently to his dualism so far as to admit that the mind cannot originate motion in the brain. That would be a veritable creation of motion out of nothing by a mere fiat of the will. It would also be in direct conflict with Descartes' physical principle that only motion can produce motion, and that the sum of motion in nature is constant, and cannot be added to. Yet incomprehensible as is the action of mind on body, that does not prevent Descartes from most emphatically asserting that it takes place. "That the mind, which is incorporeal, is capable of moving the body, neither general reasoning, nor comparisons drawn from other things, can teach us, yet none the less we cannot doubt it, since so certain and so evident experiences make it manifest to us every day of our lives." [1] [2]

Among the facts that thus make 'manifest' the incomprehensible, the most important are the feelings and passions. Had we only intellectual faculties, we should perceive any bodily injury in a purely intellectual way, as a captain perceives any damage to his

[1] *Lett.* x. p. 161, cf. also *Lett.* IX pp. 132-4.

[2] Some of Descartes' successors, however, Clauberg for instance (cf. *Corporis et Animae Conjunctio*, cap XVI.), did attempt by an analogy drawn from the material world to explain the action of mind on body. The driver of a wagon does not move the wagon, but only directs the motion of the horses that pull it. So, too, the mind needs not to cause motion in the brain, but only to direct the 'animal spirits' that already exist in the brain and are continually circling about in it. This analogy, however, as has often been pointed out, is quite misleading, since to be applicable at all to the relation between mind and body, the driver of the wagon would have to guide the movements of the horses by his mere wish. That the mind should divert a motion of the brain in a new direction is not a whit less mysterious nor less at variance with Descartes' physical teaching than that it should originate an entirely new motion. Leibniz (*Essais de Theodicée*, sec. 60, Gerhardt, VI. pp. 135-6), and also many modern commentators, assert that Descartes himself tried to escape the difficulty in this way. But though Descartes frequently speaks of the motion of the 'animal spirits' as being merely directed (not originated) by the movements of the pineal gland, he never, so far as we are aware, suggests that those movements of the pineal gland, which are involved in voluntary action, can be explained in a similar manner as previously existing and merely guided by the mind.

ship. It is the facts of pleasure and pain, and the emotions, that show the relation between mind and body to be closer and quite other than this. "Nature teaches me by these sensations of pain, hunger, thirst, etc., that I am not only lodged in my body as a pilot in a vessel, but that I am besides so intimately conjoined, and, as it were, intermixed with it, that my mind and body compose a certain unity. For if this were not the case I should not feel pain when my body is hurt, seeing I am merely a thinking thing, but should perceive the wound by the understanding alone, just as a pilot perceives by sight that part of his vessel is damaged."[1] The feelings and passions are thus the real ground of the knowledge we have of our dual nature, and to explain them mind and body must be admitted to be, as Descartes says, 'fused.' They reveal, therefore, the inadequacy of his dualism, for if he fails to account for the interaction of soul and body in sense-perception and in volition, much more must he fail to explain what he regards as their still closer union in feeling and emotion.[2]

---

[1] *Medit.* VI. (I. p. 336), Veitch's trans. p. 160.

[2] Descartes' treatise on the emotions is a good example of how little the defects in his metaphysics interfere with the excellence

Though Descartes thus inconsistently and vainly attempts to escape occasionalism, the inevitable consequences of his rationalism are one and all emphasised by his successor, Malebranche. We find nothing, Malebranche insists,[1] in the conception of any finite thing which gives us the right to think that it can act on, and produce effects in, other things. This assumed power is a fiction, and therefore every philosopher has been able to conceive it as he pleased, some by substantial forms, some by special powers or faculties, others by figure and motion; all of them alike, however, taking it as a fact proved by sense-experience that when one ball

of his scientific treatment of particular problems, for the treatise is remarkable alike in its psychological analysis of the emotions, and in the treatment of their physiological conditions.

[1] Cf. *Eclaircissement sur chap. iii. pt. ii. liv. vi. de la Recherche*: "There are many reasons which prevent me from attributing to *secondary* or *natural* causes, a force, a power, an efficacy to produce any effect whatsoever. But the chief reason is that this opinion does not seem to me even conceivable. However I may strive to comprehend it, I fail to find in me any idea that can represent the force or power that is attributed to created things." Indeed, that is a most obvious consequence of Descartes' position. If we cannot find in the conception of a material body anything which can justify us in ascribing to it the power of maintaining itself in existence, *a fortiori* we cannot hope to find in it anything that would represent the power to modify the existence of other bodies.

strikes another it sets it in motion. But this pretended demonstration *fait pitié*, Malebranche declares,[1] since it reveals the feebleness of the human mind, that even philosophers do not know that it is reason that must be consulted, and not those senses whose function consists only in revealing what is needful for the preservation of life. "When I see one ball strike another, my eyes tell me, or seem to tell me, that it is the true cause of the motion that it impresses on it; but that is only because the true cause of motion in bodies does not appear to my eyes. When I interrogate my reason I see clearly that as bodies are not able to move themselves, and as their motive force is solely the will of God, who preserves them successively in different places,[2] they cannot communicate a power that they do not possess, and that they could not communicate it even if they had it at their disposal. For the mind will never conceive how a body purely passive can transmit to another the power that transports it, whatever that power may be." Though God has established as the first law of motion, that bodies once in motion continue

[1] *Loc. cit.* Cf. also *Méditations Chrétiennes*, vi. p. 67.

[2] Cf. *Méditations Chrétiennes*, v. p. 54 : "Qui les crée ou qui les conserve successivement en différents lieux."

to move in a straight line, that does not mean that bodies of themselves persist in motion. *Bodies have no more inherent power of continuing in motion than of continuing in existence.* It means only that *God maintains and 'moves' each body by creating it anew successively in different places.* Malebranche, that is to say, denies the reality of motion altogether, save as miraculously determined change. God is not only the first, but also the sole Mover. "When I consult reason I recognise clearly that my senses mislead me, and that it is God *qui fait tout en toutes choses.*" [1] And since even within the material world all change is due to God, it does not require special proof that the interaction of mind and matter is also inconceivable, and that feelings, sensations, and ideas, have the same miraculous origin.[2]

[1] *Loc. cit.* Cf. *Entretiens*, VII. pp. 159-60, 162.

[2] Regis similarly distinguishes between the geometrical and the dynamical aspects of motion (*Cours Entier : Physique*, liv. I. pt. II. chap. IV). Like De la Forge and Malebranche, he concludes that God is the sole cause of motion on impact. " When the body *A* moves the body *B*, it is not by producing in it a new force, but by determining God, who moved the body *A*, to commence to move the body *B*"—*Ibid.* chap. VI. As regards the interaction of soul and body, De la Forge still holds that the human will is the direct and efficient cause of voluntary movements. Since Regis and Clauberg in a similar manner ascribe to the mind a directive power, Cordemoy and Geulincx must

Thus only, then, can Descartes, when consistent, make the transition from his geometry to his physics. Everything that is in nature over and above its mere

be regarded as the first consistent and thorough occasionalists. (Cf. the article by Stein—*Zur Genesis des Occasionalismus*—in the *Archiv für Geschichte der Philosophie*, I. p. 53.)   As we have not been able to procure a sight of Cordemoy's first and chief work —*Dissertations Philosophiques sur le Discernement du Corps et de l'Ame* (pub. 1666)—we give a sentence from it that is quoted by Bouillier (*Histoire de la Philosophie Cartesienne* (3rd edition), chap. XXIV. pp. 515-6): "To consider the matter exactly, it seems to me that we should not find the action of mind on body more inconceivable than that of body on mind; for we recognise that if our souls cannot move our bodies, bodies are just as incapable of moving other bodies; and as we should recognise that the meeting of two bodies is an occasion upon which the power that moved the first moves the second, we should have no difficulty in conceiving that our will is an occasion upon which the power that already moves a body directs its motion in a certain direction corresponding to our thought."   Stein states evidence, in the article above quoted, to show that though Cordemoy's *Dissertations* were published in 1666, that is to say, a year later than the first part of the *Ethica* of Geulincx, Cordemoy had already developed his views as early as 1658.   It was, however, by Geulincx that Occasionalism was first elaborated into a system.   From his fundamental principle, that a cause can only produce that which it *knows* how to produce—*impossibile est ut· is faciat qui nescit quomodo fiat*— it at once follows that spirit is the only conceivable agent, and that as the human soul, though conscious, is ignorant how bodily movements are brought about, it cannot be the cause even of its voluntary actions.   Cf. *Metaphysica Vera*, I. Quinta Scientia (Land's ed. II. p. 150).   The first volume of Malebranche's *Recherche* was published in 1674, and the second in 1675.

extendedness, all individuality and all change, have to be traced to, and find their sole ground in, the miraculous intervention of God. Nature is not explained, but explained away. The conceptual theory of mathematical knowledge may conceal its defects so long as it is tested only by those facts in the light of which it has been formulated, but immediately we come with it to the treatment of the sensible there is a complete breakdown.

Turning now to the conceptions involved in our apprehension of the mental, let us see whether Descartes here applies his rationalistic ideal with any better success. These conceptions are mind, which he identifies with consciousness or thought, imagination, and sense. Since imagination and sense are as completely distinct in nature and origin from thought,[1] as motion is from matter, Descartes again resorts to the vague term 'mode' to describe their relation to their common attribute. The term 'mode' he also uses to define the relation to thought of particular *conceptions*, and the special difficulties resulting therefrom we shall note immediately.

Already in the *Regulae*, as still more emphatically later in the *Meditations*, Descartes takes intelligence

[1] See Appendix *B* at the end of this chapter, pp. 124 ff.

as that which is alone ultimate in our knowledge.
"We can know nothing," he says in the *Regulae*,[1]
"until we know intelligence, for the knowledge of all
things depends on it, and not it on this knowledge."
Or, as he expresses it in the *Meditations*, all forms of
perception, imagination, and conception, that is, all
forms of knowledge are forms of consciousness or
thinking, and hence consciousness is known in knowing anything.   And he adds in the *Meditations*, that
mind is therefore better known than matter.

Now thought or consciousness is used in two senses
by Descartes.   Sometimes it is used as a general name
for all states of consciousness.   All the *contents* of
consciousness, as ideas or states of the self, are known
directly face to face, and are necessarily such as they
appear to the mind to be.   And on this view the unconditioned nature of consciousness is shared in by
all its ultimate and irreducible contents.   These
contents, indeed, are regarded as being identical with
it, and the necessary expression of its nature.   "All
the sciences united are nothing but the human
understanding "—the rest of the sentence, however,
indicates the want of clearness in Descartes' view
of consciousness — "All   the   sciences   united   are

[1] *Reg.* viii. (xi. p. 243).

nothing but the human understanding, *whose light* remains one and the same whatever be the *objects* to which it applies itself."[1]   Consciousness is here distinguished from its contents.   They are its objects, and it is but the light by which they are revealed to the mind.[2]   It is in this way, as an ultimate unanalysable simple force or light, that Descartes conceives consciousness, when he takes it as one member, of his dualism and defines it in opposition to extension. ⟨When regarded as expressing itself in and through its innate ideas, and therefore partially in and through the conceptions of matter and motion, it obviously cannot be so defined in opposition to them.   And to have attempted to define it in abstraction from all its contents, when indeed it is the merest abstraction, is another of the fundamental errors of the Cartesian philosophy.[3]

[1] *Reg.* I. (XI. p. 202).   The latter part of the sentence is condensed in order to bring out more clearly its essential meaning. The complete translation is given in the chapter on Descartes' Method, p. 22.

[2] Cf. Norris : *Theory of the Ideal World*, II. pp. 113-4.

[3] While Descartes thus in his metaphysics takes consciousness as a simple unanalysable light, Kant regards the unity of consciousness as, of all things in the universe, the most complex, since it involves irreducibly in its unity the distinction of subject and object, the object again involving the element of

If now we first follow Malebranche in his criticism of Descartes, and see how space (even 'intelligible' space) with all its contents is the object of mind and not a modification or state of it, is not a self but a not-self, and so clear up the ambiguities involved in Descartes' use of the term 'mode' to denote the relation of the objects of mind to itself,[1] we shall then be able to bring to a clear issue the question whether or not Descartes is justified in asserting that mind is better known than matter.

Malebranche has no difficulty in showing that Descartes, on his own principles, cannot assert that the mind knows extension by perceiving it in itself, as a state or modification of itself. We can conceive extension alone without thinking of any other thing, and we can never conceive modes without conceiving the subject of which they are the modes. And not

space, and implying the categories of substance and causality. By means of this analysis of Descartes' ultimate, Kant provides a sure basis for the rationalism which Descartes fails to found, and solves many problems which for Descartes and his successors had been insoluble. The Cartesian views of consciousness are treated more at length in Appendix *D* at the end of this chapter, p. 133.

[1] We must see how ideas cannot any more than motion be regarded as modes, and that just as figure is the only possible modification of extension, so feeling is the only known modification of mind.

only do we thus conceive extension without thinking of mind, we cannot even conceive how it could be a modification of mind. We can conceive space as limited, and so as having figure, and that mind cannot have. We must also conceive it as divisible into parts, and we see nothing in mind that is so divisible. And lastly, while space is infinite, the self is finite. For all these reasons, space cannot be seen in mind, and, therefore, cannot be a modification of it.[1] The mind cannot contain extension without itself becoming extended, and, what is more, infinite in extent.[2]

Also, we have only to appeal to our experience to assure ourselves that when we apprehend extension, we apprehend something distinct from the self. When we perceive the sun for instance, though we cannot see the actual material sun, since it is not in itself knowable, that which we do see, and with which the mind

[1] Malebranche adds also the further argument, that we can think on a circle or triangle in general, though it is a contradiction that the soul, which is a particular thing, should have a modification in general.

[2] Cf. *Méditations Chrétiennes*, i. p. 13 : "Do you think you have sufficient scope to contain in yourself even that which you can conceive in what is called an atom ; for you conceive clearly that the smallest part of matter that you imagine, being infinitely divisible, potentially includes an infinity of different figures and relations." The study of Augustine brought this difficulty home to Malebranche.

is immediately united, we perceive clearly to be something distinct from us ; and therefore we fly in the face of all the evidence (" *contre notre lumière et contre notre conscience* ") when we say that the mind sees in its own modifications all the objects that it perceives.[1]

Separating, then, from the mind all ideas in which space is involved as being the objects of mind and non-mental, what is left on the mental side ?   Malebranche answers, and we must agree with him, nothing but feelings.   "Pleasure, pain, taste, heat, colour, all our sensations, and all our passions, are modifications of the mind " [2]   They are not involved in the conception of matter, and as it would be impiety to ascribe them to God, arguing by exclusion, we must refer them to the mind.   And in spite of the differences between sensations and emotions, they must (since we in no

[1] *Eclaircissement sur chap. viii. pt. ii. liv. iii. de la Recherche.*   It will be noted that the above criticism presupposes that *conceptions* are *objects* of mind, and it is in that way that Descartes also views them (cf. in this chapter, pp. 108-9), saving on the few occasions when he interprets consciousness in the first and non-dualistic manner.   Either, then, his dualistic view of consciousness as the opposite of extension must be given up, which would involve the complete transformation of his system ; or this criticism of Malebranche must be granted as unanswerable. Cf. below, Appendix *D*, p. 133.

[2] *Loc. cit.*

case know them) be all alike called feelings. Can we compare heat with taste, odour with colour, or even one colour with another?[1] With these modes of mind it is not as with figures, that being known in conception can be compared one with another and their relations clearly recognised. Between those intelligible figures, which are clear and distinct ideas, and these modes of mind, which are only confused feelings, there is no community. And that being so, why, Malebranche asks, pretend that those intelligible figures can only be known if they are modes of mind, when the mind knows none of what alone undoubtedly are its modes by clear conception, but only by inner sense?[2] Instead of the sensations and feelings being related to mind, as Descartes would fain make out, as motion is to matter, and pure conceptions being its proper modes, it is just the reverse.

If Descartes is to separate, as in his metaphysics he continually does, ideas (taking ideas in the strict sense as distinguished from feelings) from the mind, and to define the consciousness, whereby they are supposed to be revealed to mind, as the opposite of that element of extension, which is the fundamental and only real

[1] Cf. *Réponse à Arnauld*, chap. VIII.
[2] " Par conscience ou par sentiment interieur," *loc. cit.*

element in all of them,[1] then of course the above criticism of Malebranche is unanswerable.[2] Consciousness cannot contain its opposite as a state of itself, nor indeed know it at all, unless God be again regarded as miraculously intervening, and presenting to mind what could never otherwise be known by it.[3]

[1] Malebranche's proof that, on Cartesian principles, strictly interpreted, we can have no ‘ideas’ of the spiritual, will be given immediately.

[2] The same criticism was made by Gassendi in his excellent *Objections* to Descartes' *Méditations*, and Descartes in his reply carefully avoids the main issue.

[3] Malebranche's own solution, that we know space by participation in God's knowledge of it, explains nothing, for the same difficulty recurs with the same force in the case of God. How can space exist in the mind of God without God becoming thereby material ? That difficulty, which he could not solve, he escapes by asserting the unknowableness of God. " God includes in Himself the perfections of matter without being material . . . He possesses also the perfections of created spirits, without being spirit, in the manner we conceive spirit : his true name is, *He that is,* that is to say, Being without restriction, All Being, Being infinite and universal." *Recherche*, liv. III. pt. II. chap. IX., at the end. Cf. *Entretiens*, VIII. p. 185. The futility of Regis' reply to Malebranche, in defence of their common master, is an interesting demonstration of the unanswerableness of Malebranche's criticisms. Regis admits that the mind cannot know space of itself and by its own natural powers, since not being extended, extension does not belong to its essence. But after proving that no known faculty will account for the appearance of extension in mind, he concludes by exclusion that it must belong to the essence of *soul* as distinguished from mind, and

Now, as a consequence of this removal of the objective content of knowledge to the not-self, it follows that so far is Descartes' contention that the mind is better known than matter from being true, that it must now be admitted that it is not known at all, but only felt.[1] When Descartes asserts that that therefore the *soul* knows it by itself, and by its own proper nature. (*Cours Entier de Philosophie*: *la Metaph.* liv. II. pt. I. chap. III.) Soul (*l'âme*) he distinguishes from mind (*l'esprit*) as being the mind temporarily modified by its union with the body. Experience teaches us, he says, that it is one of the laws established by the Author of Nature, that the mind (*l'esprit*), so long as it is united to the body, have the idea of extension (*Ibid.* liv. I. pt. II. chap. VI.). It is in accordance with this condition that the soul (*l'âme*) thinks always on some body. But how it is possible for the mind thus to be modified Regis makes no attempt to explain. The empirical fact, spite of its inexplicability, is ultimately his sole reply to Malebranche's and Gassendi's criticism. The problem of how the unextended mind can know extension remains as insoluble for Descartes and Malebranche as for Augustine. Cf. Norris: *Theory of the Ideal World*, I. pp. 295-7. Arnauld (cf. Appendix *A*, p. 115) asserts that it is as ridiculous to ask how the mind, whose essence consists in the power of perception, can perceive objects, as to demand how matter can be divisible or have figure (*Des Vraies et des Fausses Idées*, chap. II.). He forgets that consciousness has been defined as the opposite of extension, while extension has not been defined as the opposite of divisibility or of figure. Also, while our knowledge of extension is clear and distinct, we have, as Malebranche and Hume both show, no distinct knowledge of mind ; and still less, if that be possible, of any 'faculty' or 'power' of mind.

[1] Even the fact of the self's *existence* is, Malebranche holds, not

we know it completely, and even better (the over - emphasis is significant) than extension, he is viewing consciousness in the dualistic manner as a simple unanalysable light, and therefore as better known in its simplicity than is the extension that requires a science of geometry to unfold its inexhaustible multiplicity.[1]   As all forms of knowledge are forms of it, must it not, Descartes asks, be known in knowing anything ?   This, however, according to Malebranche, does not follow : that by which all things are known need not be itself known.[2]   As

known, but only felt.   Though universal axioms are recognised through the intuition of particular quantities, the same can hardly be said of the universal truth, that all consciousness involves existence, for the assurance, which the self has of being conscious at a particular moment, is not an 'intuition' in the sense of being the apprehension of necessary relation between particular given quantities, but only the immediate assurance in feeling of a contingent fact.   This is likewise emphasised by Leibniz.   Cf. *Nouveaux Essais*, liv. IV. chap. II. sec. 1, also chap. VII. sec. 7 (Gerhardt, v. pp. 347-8 and 391-2).   And to such criticism Descartes cannot reply.   Since, on his own admission, existence (save as regards the Divine Being) falls altogether outside the sphere of rational knowledge, the self's existence can be no exception.   The ambiguities involved in Malebranche's use of the term 'feeling,' as not knowledge and yet a form of knowing, we cannot here discuss.

[1] That too, doubtless, would be Descartes' answer to the question why, if mind is better known than matter, there is no science of it corresponding to the mathematical sciences.

[2] This contention of Malebranche certainly holds against

Augustine points out, the eyes, by which we see all things, cannot see themselves directly, and, if there were no mirrors, would never see themselves at all. The absence of the knowledge to which Descartes here pretends is well brought out by Malebranche's English disciple, Norris: "What this formal thought or perception is, as to the reality of the thing, you will ask me in vain, because 'tis in vain that I ask myself. I know, or rather feel by inward sentiment that I think, and I make a shift in a rational method to find out what it is that thinks in me; but what that act of mine which I call *thinking* is, I want, I will not say words to express, but penetration of thought to comprehend. Sometimes my fancy whispers me that 'tis a kind of application of the mind to its ideal or intelligible object; but then I reject that again as a figurative way of speaking, borrowed from the position or conservation of one body to another. Then, again, I say to myself, that sure 'tis an intellectual sight, a kind of vision of the mind. But here I correct myself again, as soon as I consider the meaning of what I say. . . . But what then shall I say that it is? Or without offering at

Descartes, so long as Descartes interprets consciousness abstractly as something real apart from its contents.

anything further, shall I own my ignorance ? That I find I must do, since there is no seeing without light. I enter into myself again and again, I consult myself over and over, but can have no answer." [1]

Indirectly the same conclusion may be proved in three ways. First, this consciousness that is supposed to be so clearly known can only be defined by negatives, all of which gain meaning through that opposite, extension, which is asserted to be the less clearly known. It is defined by Descartes as *un*extended and *in*divisible. Though he adds the positive predicate ' active,' that is just what later he shows that consciousness is not; [2] and being therefore forced to introduce an obscure faculty of will, distinct from thought, he destroys what little clearness was remaining in his analysis of mind.

Secondly, the indirect manner in which Descartes proves the secondary qualities to be modes of mind, [3] itself indicates our ignorance of mind. " Since we are obliged to consult the idea of extension, in order to

[1] Norris: *The Theory of the Ideal World* (pub. 1704), vol. II. pp. 109-10.

[2] Cf. below, pp. 108 ff.

[3] Descartes' argument is that, as they are not involved in our idea of extension, they must belong to the only other substantial form of existence, viz., mind.

discover whether the sensible qualities are modes of mind, is it not evident that we have no clear idea of mind ? Otherwise would we think of taking this roundabout road ? When a philosopher wishes to discover whether figure belongs to extension, does he consult the idea of mind or any idea save that of extension ? Does he not see clearly in the very idea of extension that figure is a modification of it ? And would it not be absurd if, to enlighten himself, he argued thus : there are two kinds of existence, mind and matter, figure is not a mode of mind, therefore it is a mode of matter ? " [1]

From this unavoidable acceptance of the feelings and sensations as modes of mind Malebranche draws his third argument for its unknowableness. As they are modes of mind, they must be deducible from the conception of mind, just as the different figures and their necessary relations are deducible from the idea of that of which they are the modifications. But since it is obvious that no such deduction can be made, and that (as was pointed out above[2]) between the different sensations and feelings no relations can be perceived, the conclusion

---

[1] *Eclaircissement sur chap. vii. pt. ii. liv. iii. de la Recherche.*
[2] p. 95.

is unavoidable that the archetypal idea of mind,
upon which they are dependent, is unknown to us.
"Without this archetypal idea of mind I cannot
know that I am capable of feeling the taste of
melon, the sensation of red, the pain of toothache,
unless I have actually experienced these feelings:
feelings, I say, that are confused and make themselves felt, without making either themselves or the
substances which they modify known."[1]   To the

[1] *Réponse à Arnauld*, chap. XIII. Cf. Norris : *Theory of the
Ideal World*, II. pp. 213-5 : " What the nature of that pleasure
or pain is which we feel . . . that we know no more of than
if we had never felt either of them.   Not but that this is an
intelligible thing, because God knows it, and we ourselves may
possibly know it hereafter, when we come to have a sight (a
great and engaging sight indeed) of that *archetypal idea*, upon
which our souls were formed. . . .   I need not scruple to say
that he that can *see* knows no more of light or colour than he
that is *blind*."   This tendency to regard the sensations of the
secondary qualities as illusory appearances of intelligible realities
runs through the whole Cartesian school.   At times Spinoza and
Leibniz even speak as if they regarded sound, light, and colour,
as illusions that would completely vanish on perfected knowledge.   Geulincx alone, of all the Cartesians, insists on
their intrinsic reality and worth.   Cf. Geulincx's *Annotata ad
Metaphysicam* (Land's edition, II. p. 288) : "So God has
in a sense made two worlds, one in itself. . .   The other
God has made in us and in our senses, endowing it with
wonderful and most beautiful images and phantasms (*spectris
et phantasmatibus*) ; and this latter world is far more lovely and
more artistic ; in it there breathes more wisdom and goodness
than in that other world."

natural question, what such conceptual knowledge of sensations and feelings would be like, Malebranche may of course reply that as we are wholly ignorant of the nature and essence of mind, we cannot expect to be able to form any notion of what a rational science of mind, corresponding to the rational sciences of matter, would reveal.[1] Only we can assume, he adds, that as mind is a creature infinitely more perfect than matter, we should, if we knew it, in our absorption in the gradual clarification of the mysteries of mind, despise all other knowledge, even mathematics. If the properties of unintelligent space are so marvellous, so luminously interconnected and yet so inexhaustively varied, a very image of Deity in the combination of necessary unity with inexhaustible variety, what may we not expect from the unknown idea of mind?[2] "Could

---

[1] From this impossibility, in the actual limitation of our knowledge, of a rational science of mind Malebranche drew the conclusion that an empirical method is the only possible one in psychology ; and so became one of the founders of the science of empirical psychology, anticipating Berkeley in his analysis of sense-perception.

[2] *Méditations Chrétiennes*, IX. pp. 120-21 : "If a mathematician has so much delight when he compares magnitudes among themselves that he often sacrifices his pleasures and his health to find out the properties of a line . . . what pleasure would men not take in comparing among themselves by a clear

we attend to the preservation of a body that would trouble incessantly the sweet delights of contemplating the inconceivable perfections of an intelligent nature ? " [1]

And therein we find the reason, which Augustine sought in vain, why a benevolent Deity has revealed

view of the understanding so many different modifications [of their own being], of which the bare feeling, although feeble and confused, does so strangely busy and employ them. For you must know that the mind contains in itself all the beauty which you see in the world, and which you attribute to the objects which surround you. Those colours, those odours, those tastes, and an infinity of other feelings by which you have never been affected, are nothing but modifications of your substance. That harmony which carries you away is not in the air that strikes your ear, and those infinite pleasures, of which the most voluptuous have only a feeble feeling, are included in the capacity of your mind." The possible modes of mind are, Malebranche believes, like the possible modifications of extension, unlimited in number. Cf. Norris' *Ideal World*, II. pp. 259-60 : " How many more [senses] we may be capable of, if the power of the soul were wholly reduced to act, who can say ? . . . And what more [impressions] we might experience if God should create, not new organs of sense in us, but only new bodies to make different impressions upon those we have already, is a vast abyss which no line of thought can ever fathom. But then consider what a great and noble being this soul of ours is, and how large is its capacity, that carries enclosed in its single self the beauties of a whole world ; those I mean which we ascribe to it, and distribute among the several parts of it, and withal think a sufficient furniture for the adorning of that immense fabrick."

[1] *Réponse à Arnauld*, chap. XXII.

to us the knowledge of what is without us, and yet has left us in utter darkness as to what is within : our knowledge is sufficient for the perform-ance of our duties, and any further knowledge would only distract us from the work that has to be done.[1]

[1] Cf. Norris : *Theory of the Ideal World*, ii. pp. 263-4 : " Happy time indeed, when we shall know both God and ourselves, and ourselves in God, whose superlative beauty will not allow us to grow proud of our own. . . . Now our feeble eyes would be dazzled with our own light, and we should fall in love with the dear image of our own being ; but when the looking-glass shall be so much more charmingly beautiful than the face, we may then securely behold ourselves in it.   In the meantime let us esteem that the best knowledge of ourselves is to have a deep sense of our infirmities, and not be ashamed of that ignorance which is the guardian of our humility."   Perhaps, too, it might be suggested, we have here the explanation of Augustine's problem, how we should know the stars so far above us, and yet remain ignorant of the bodily processes ' within' us.   We have the knowledge which we require (the modern theory of evolution explaining further the reason why), and no other.

From our knowledge of extension Malebranche derives even such knowledge of mind as is required to prove its independence of body and its immortality.   (Cf. *Réponse à Arnauld*, chap. XXIII. and also *Méditations Chrétiennes*, IX. p. 122.)   Descartes' reply to Gassendi, when the latter made the same objection, that the substance of the self is not known, is utterly helpless.   (Cf. Gassendi's *Objections to the Meditations*, and Descartes' reply thereto.)   For Regis' defence of Descartes, cf. *Cours Entier* : *la Metaph.* liv. II. pt. I. chap. VI.

Now, such a romantic conception of the possibilities of rational science, which significantly reappears in the English matter-of-fact Locke,[1] cannot be put aside as a mystic dream of the Malebranche that is a follower of Plato and Augustine. it is also the natural extension of the rationalism of Descartes. Either there is a limit set to his rationalism in sense, with a resulting dualism between the intelligible and the sensible,[2] or such a deduction of the sensations and feelings from the conception of mind is as possible as is the deduction of mathematical truths from the conception of space. This application, however, of the mistaken conception of mathematical method to mind and its states, brings out the fantastic nature of the rationalism that necessitates such a conclusion. It appears to the undiscerning mind possible enough from the conception of space, or at least from the conceptions of the different figures in space, by sheer power of reasoning to deduce all

[1] Cf. *Essay* : IV. III. 27, and IV. XII. 12.

[2] Descartes only kept this difficulty out of sight by a persistent ignoring of sense, and an alternate reference of it now to matter and now to mind. If we keep to his criterion of truth, and to his presupposed doctrine of essence, this theory of Malebranche of a rational science of mind is the only possible outlet.

the content of geometrical science, but the illusion wears thin, and the teaching becomes doubtful, when in like manner the possibility is asserted of deducing from the conception of mind all the various sensations and feelings that we experience in it. We see how long a road it is from such a rationalism to the rationalism of Kant : we are still under the influence of the mystic idealism of Plato.[1]

Thus we come to the general conclusion that, alike in the metaphysics of matter and in the metaphysics of mind, Descartes' rationalism reveals its inadequacy, for while in the one we are brought to an irresolvable dualism between the geometrical and the mechanical,

[1] Malebranche's rationalism ought consistently to be carried yet further. Since souls are modifications of consciousness, the different souls and their relations to one another must be deducible, as well as the content of each separate soul. The idea from which deduction must start is not the idea of a particular concrete self, which as concrete and particular is complex and derivative, but the simple, and therefore ultimate, idea of consciousness in general. Thus impossible as Malebranche's rationalism seems, it is outdone by that of Spinoza who takes that last step. The perpetual interchange of the most simple with the most complex, to which Cartesian thinking was condemned, is here again apparent. It is also illustrated in the position of Leibniz. Regarding the idea of the individual soul as the datum from which deduction must proceed, he is forced to infer that it involves in its content the notion of the whole universe.

in the other we reach a similar dualism of thought and sense. And if we follow him a step further, while he states the relation in which he regards thought as standing to its intelligible contents, when, that is, he approaches the problem seriously, and ceases to pretend to dismiss it by the conveniently indefinite term 'mode,' we shall see how he is forced not only to recognise the limitations of his rationalism, but also to undermine its very foundations.

Thought, Descartes emphasises, is purely passive in knowledge, being governed wholly by its objects.[1] If, he says,[2] I conceive a triangle, even supposing there is not and never was in any place in the universe apart from my thought any such figure, nevertheless it remains true that the conception possesses a certain determinate immutable nature or essence, which is not framed by me, and is not in any way dependent on my individual thinking. Though the mind is free to

---

[1] Cf. *Lett.* IX. p. 166: "I do not distinguish otherwise between mind and its ideas than between a piece of wax and the different figures that it can receive ; and as it is not properly an action, but a passion in the wax to receive different figures, it seems to me that it is also a passion in the mind to receive such and such an idea, and that only its volitions are actions." Cf. *Lett.* VIII. p. 513.

[2] *Médit.* v. at the beginning.

think or not to think such ideas, once thought they
control and govern our minds, there being in each
of them a necessity that forces us to develop it in
one particular way. It is thus that conceptions
separate themselves out from the subjective life of
feeling and imagination, and set themselves over
against the mind as something objective.[1]

That, then, is the fact : how is it to be explained ?
How is it possible that the mind should *at will*
bring into consciousness ideas which yet it has not
formed or created, and over whose development it has
no control ? Descartes' answer is that they must
have been implanted in the mind by God. They
are innate, and therefore the mind has not to form
them, but simply by its attention to throw on them
the light of consciousness.[2] The understanding is

---

[1] Note how entirely Descartes agrees with Malebranche that
conceptions are *objects* of mind.

[2] Malebranche's objections (*Recherche*, liv. III. pt. II. chap IV.
p. 390 ff.) to this position are, first, that it would involve the
existence of an infinitely infinite number of ideas in the finite
mind ; and, secondly, that even if the mind had stored up in it
all these ideas, it would be impossible to explain how it could
at any moment find among them those it wanted. The kinship
of Descartes' position to the monadism of Leibniz may be noted.
How near Descartes can yet at times come to Malebranche's
own position appears from the following : "Intuitive knowledge
is an illumination of the mind by God, by which it sees in the

purely passive alike in the reception of its innate ideas and in their development. All we need to do is to keep our minds fixed on them, and out of them spontaneously all truth will arise.[1]

light of God the things which he pleases to reveal to it, by a direct impression of the divine clearness on our understanding, which in that is not considered as agent, but only as receiving the rays of the divine Being " (*Lett.* x. p. 130).

[1] It is because Descartes regards the mind as passive in thinking, that the problem of accounting for error is felt so strongly by him, and is dwelt upon at such length in the fourth *Meditation* and in the *Principles*. If God cannot deceive us, and is the ultimate source of ideas, must not all our ideas be true and error impossible? Descartes' reply is that error never lies in our ideas, but only in the judgments which we make about them. And according to Descartes all judgment is an act of the will. Though the understanding furnishes the ideas, before these ideas, which are but subjective appearances in the mind, can become knowledge, the will must intervene and confer upon them by affirmation that objective reference which in themselves they do not possess. If the understanding alone conceives, the will alone affirms. Truth is the united product of the understanding and the will. Now since the faculty of will is the faculty of a rational being, the active side of a mind whose essence consists in pure thought, its activities ought to be guided by the understanding. The will, however, being infinite (cf. below, p. 113) rouses in us an infinite desire for knowledge. And error arises when, impelled by this desire, we do not restrain the will within the same limits as the understanding, but give our assent or denial also to those ideas of which we have only an obscure and confused apprehension. Error thus consists in a wrong use of the freedom of the will. All deception is self-deception.

In order to make out the opposition to matter
Descartes has to take the self as active, and on its
activity he all along insists. But now that he has
shown the mind in thinking to be passive, he has
either to deny that it is really any more active than
material bodies, or to withdraw his definition of
its essence as consisting in pure thought, and in pure
thought alone.[1] This internal dialectic of his system
is reinforced, and the alternative to be chosen decided

---

[1] Here again Malebranche is the more consistent Cartesian,
though, of course, as a student of Augustine, he would be pre-
disposed to question the freedom of the will. " Will is a
property which always accompanies the mind, be it united with
the body or be it separate from it ; but yet it is not essential to
it, since it presupposes thought, and we can conceive a mind
without will, just as we can conceive a body without motion "
(*Recherche*, liv. III. pt. I. chap. I. p. 342).   Will is as externally
related to mind as motion is to matter. " Not only are bodies
incapable of being the true causes of anything whatsoever, spirits
the most noble are equally powerless. They can know nothing
unless God enlightens them. They can feel nothing unless
God affects them. They are capable of willing nothing
unless God moves them towards the good in general, that is to
say, towards himself " (*Ibid.* liv. VI. pt. II. chap. III. p. 327).
His fifth *Meditation* (p. 50) opens with the prayer, " Increase my
love for the truth, in order that my attention be renewed, and
that you may grant this natural prayer after you have formed it
in me." Malebranche's attempt, in spite of these admissions,
still to vindicate the freedom of the will is sincere but sophistical.   It is interesting to compare Malebranche's view of the
self both with that of Spinoza and with that of Hume.

for him, by the emphasis laid on the will in the religious thought of his time. Being always careful to respect, even in minor matters, the doctrines of the Church, he not only conforms to the theological doctrine of the freedom of the will in all its absoluteness, but insists on it in a way that shows his conformity to be complete.[1] To it he is ready to sacrifice his most cherished convictions, even his rationalism.

Since thought is passive, necessarily the will must be altogether different from it. If the will were identical with thought, or determined by it, it would like thought be determined by an impersonal authority outside and above the self, and so would not be will at all, not anything which could express the reality of the self as an independent agent. In this way Descartes, immediately after having declared that the whole essence of the self consists in pure thought, is forced inconsistently to assert that it is something quite distinct from thought that forms its essence, namely, an inconceivable occult will.[2] The power

[1] Cf. *Principles*, i. 39 (iii. pp. 86-7).

[2] The contradiction Descartes conceals by the assertion that thought reveals itself as being of a twofold nature, at once active and passive. *Principles*, i. 32 (iii. p. 83). Cf. *Lett.* viii. pp. 275 and 513, where he asserts that action and passion are one and the same thing. Cf. also below, pp. 135-6.

of will alone of all faculties in us is infinite and perfect,[1] the necessary truths of reason being but an *external* limit set to it by God.[2]

Also, as a further consequence, he had to interpret the nature of God in the same impossible way. Ideas, and the 'necessary' truths of reason which they involve, cannot be regarded, Descartes holds, as the objects of divine thought, for in that case they would be an alien necessity governing God's mind just as they do ours, and we should thereby commit the

[1] *Médit.* IV. (I. pp. 300-2) Veitch's trans. pp. 137-8 : "If I consider the faculty of understanding which I possess, I find that it is of very small, extent and greatly limited. . . . In the same way if I examine the faculty of memory or imagination, or any other faculty I possess, I find none that is not small and circumscribed. . . . It is the faculty of will only, or freedom of choice, which I experience to be so great that I am unable to conceive the idea of another that shall be more ample and extended ; so that it is chiefly my will which leads me to discern that I bear a certain image and similitude of Deity." Cf. *ibid.* p. 140 : "As the will consists only of a single element, and that indivisible, it would appear that this faculty is of such a nature that nothing could be taken from it [without destroying it]." Spinoza gives an interesting, and very complete, criticism of Descartes' doctrine of the will. *Ethica*, II. 49, *Scholium* ; cf. below, chap. IV. pp. 138-9, and note to p. 139.

[2] That God, through the innate ideas which He has implanted in the mind, should concur with us in forming our acts of will, is, Descartes is careful to add (*loc. cit.* pp. 140-1), no cause of complaint, "since those acts are wholly good and true, in so far as they depend on God."

absurdity of subjecting God "to destiny and Styx."[1]
The ideas of God's mind, and the 'eternal' truths of
reason which they involve, must be regarded as
created by God, and therefore as wholly dependent
on His will:—though how God's mind could exist
without ideas over against it, any more than ours
could, Descartes did not stop to inquire.   As Norris
remarks, Descartes conceives God as working in
darkness to create the light.   "For if even necessary
truth be the effect of God, then antecedently to the
effecting of it there was no truth, and consequently
no knowledge, because nothing knowable.   And so
God in the production of truth (if, indeed, He did
produce it) must be supposed to act in the dark, and
without intelligence to order even an intellectual
system."[2]   Thus does Descartes' rationalism, after
showing itself to be inadequate to the treatment of the
real, either as matter or as mind, end in the suicidal
admission of the absolute relativity of all knowledge.
His rationalism, which gave as answer to the problem
of the limits of knowledge, that there are none, and
that the material and the mental are alike transparent
to us, changes into a complete agnosticism.

[1] *Lett.* vi. p. 109.
[2] Norris; *Theory of the Ideal World*, i. p. 337.   Cf. pp. 343 ff.

In Descartes' system, then, as we have tried to show, there are three fundamental tenets, viz., the doctrine of representative perception, a very peculiar form of rationalism, and the conception of spirit as an active creative agency.   In these three doctrines his whole system may be regarded as summed up.   The dualism, which forms his problem, inevitably gave rise to the first ; from his studies in mathematics he derived the second ; and by the third (based on immediate experience, but interpreted chiefly in the light of certain scholastic principles) he constructs a completed system, spite of all the insoluble difficulties in which he is landed by the first two.   We shall seek, in the following chapters, to confirm this inter-pretation of Descartes' teaching by an examination of these three fundamental principles as they re-appear in the systems of his successors.

APPENDICES TO CHAPTER III.

A[1]—ARNAULD'S DENIAL OF THE DOCTRINE OF REPRESENTATIVE PERCEPTION.

THE only thinker within the early Cartesian School who called in question the doctrine of representative

[1] To p. 52, above.

perception was Arnauld.   In his *Traité des Vraies et des Fausses Idées*,[1] which was written as a criticism of Malebranche's *Recherche de la Verité*, he states in the most definite manner that there is no direct evidence of the existence of subjective states, acting as intermediaries between mind and matter, and that the sole (and on his view insufficient) ground for their assumption is (as we have already seen in the Chapter on Descartes' problem) the local difference between object known and the brain through which it is known.[2]   But as Arnauld himself accepts the Cartesian dualism in all its absoluteness, his denial of this fundamental tenet of the Cartesian system comes to no fruitful result.   His assertion that the mind's faculty of knowing objects distinct from it constitutes

[1] Published in 1683.

[2] *Des Vraies et des Fausses Idées*, chap. IV.   Even the ground that objects cannot be known directly, since they are material and therefore wholly different from the immaterial mind, reduces to this one ground.   For it is because the mind is unextended, that, even though it be *locally* present to a body, it still remains external to it.   As Malebranche remarks, though the mind were to issue out of the body in order to visit the sun, being unextended it could not contain that star within itself, and would therefore, even though it got inside it, still remain as external to it as one body is to another.   Also, as Arnauld, following Augustine and Malebranche, emphasises, the mind knows least of that to which it is most closely united, namely the brain.   Cf. Arnauld, chap. VIII.

its very essence, and ought therefore to be accepted as an ultimate, is an arbitrary and dogmatic attempt to set a limit to legitimate scientific analysis.[1]   In that assertion the Cartesian assumption of the self as an abiding, simple, substantial agent again reveals itself.   It is interesting to compare Malebranche's reply to Arnauld [2] with Hume's criticism of the same theory.[3]   Reid's position is in essentials identical with that of Arnauld, the flagrant unfairness in his statement of the latter's theory [4] being indirect proof thereof.

B [5]—DESCARTES' THEORY OF PERCEPTION, AND ACCOUNT OF THE RELATION BETWEEN SENSE AND UNDERSTANDING.

THE criterion of truth Descartes first applies to the content of perception.   What is it, he asks, that we clearly and distinctly perceive when we perceive an external object ?   " Take, for example, this piece of wax ; it is quite fresh, having been but recently

[1] Cf. above, note 3 to p. 96, at the end.

[2] *Eclaircissement sur la Nature des Idées :* 1re Objection.

[3] Given below, chap. VI. pp. 228 ff.

[4] *Essays on the Intellectual Powers of Man :* Essay II. chap. XIII.

[5] To p. 62, above.

taken from the bee-hive; it has not yet lost the sweetness of the honey it contained; it still retains somewhat of the odour of the flowers from which it was gathered; its colour, figure, size, are apparent [to the sight]; it is hard, cold, easily handled; and sounds when struck upon with the finger. In fine, all that contributes to make a body as distinctly known as possible, is found in the one before us. But, while I am speaking, let it be placed near the fire—what remained of the taste exhales, the smell evaporates, the colour changes, its figure is destroyed, its size increases, it becomes liquid, it grows hot, it can hardly be handled, and although struck upon, it emits no sound. Does the same wax still remain after this change? It must be admitted that it does remain, no one doubts it, or judges otherwise." [1] What, then, is it that remains the same? It can be none of the original sensible qualities, since they have all disappeared. It must be that we distinguish in the piece of wax a body which appeared to us a moment before under these sensible qualities, and now appears to us under others: and if we remove all the changeable qualities from it, nothing remains but a body, a something, extended, flexible, and

[1] *Médit.* II. (I. pp. 256-7) Veitch's trans. pp. 110-11.

moveable.   The wax in all its possible forms, so long as it exists at all must fill space, be it a larger or be it a smaller space, for otherwise it would exist nowhere, and therefore not at all.   So too, though the number of different shapes it may take on are infinite, it must under all conditions possess some figure.   And finally, as a consequence of its being extended, it is always capable of being moved: since it is always somewhere, it can always be shifted somewhere else. These three qualities are the only qualities, which the piece of wax preserves throughout all its changes, and must therefore constitute the 'it' we refer to, when we say that 'it' remains the same spite of its transformations.   These qualities constitute the essence, the self-identity, of the piece of wax.   That argument Descartes strengthens by a second application of his criterion of truth, showing that all the other sensible qualities are known only *obscurely* and *confusedly*.   Thus to take as an example the quality, yellow.   Though as a sensation in the mind it is perfectly clear, as a quality in the wax it is in its exact nature unknown.   And further, the knowledge we have of the wax through that quality is also confused.   Colour exists in the mind, not in material things, and when we refer colour as a quality to a material thing, we confound together mind and body, the spiritual and the material. The object exists apart from our perception, and hence apart from the qualities with which we clothe it in the act of perception. The three qualities, then, of extension, figure, and motion, are alone known clearly, as they exist in the external object, and distinctly, as apart from the mind, and together must constitute its whole essence.

Descartes next proceeds to determine the relations in which these qualities stand to one another, and to the material bodies whose qualities they are; and that he does by means of the three scholastic terms, substance, attribute, and mode. As regards their relation to one another, though we can conceive extension apart from any particular figure, and apart from all motion, we cannot in a similar way conceive figure and motion apart from extension. To extension figure and motion are related, Descartes therefore concludes, as *modes* to a common *attribute*. Again, Descartes takes the relation of extension to matter as that of attribute to substance. Extension is the attribute, and, further, it is the sole attribute, of body. Matter is perfectly homogeneous; having no inner determinations or qualitative differences, its whole nature is exhausted in the fact that it fills space.

From this identification of matter and extension there follow several important consequences. First, since space is related to body as attribute to substance, and since save in substance no attribute can exist, there can be no empty space. Secondly, matter, like space, must be continuous, and therefore both infinite in divisibility and infinite in extent. Thirdly, since there cannot be different kinds of extension, there cannot be different kinds of matter. There are different planetary systems, but the material substance constituting them all is one and the same. Fourthly, it is obvious that body as thus identified with extension is purely passive. Motion must therefore have been introduced into the material world by some cause outside it, and that cause can only be God. Also, since bodies have no power to produce motion, they cannot increase or diminish it. The quantity of motion in nature therefore remains constant. And lastly, since all bodies are thus passive, with no inner forces, the only causes of motion are the external efficient causes, impact and pressure.

The material world, then, on Descartes' view is

a world that has lost all the sensible qualities under which it appears to us, and preserves only its geometrical qualities, extension and figure, and as introduced from outside, motion. Yet what the natural world loses in richness and variety, it gains in simplicity and clearness; what may appear an aesthetic loss is an intellectual gain, since instead of the confused bewildering world of the senses, we have a world in which one single phenomenon, motion in space, infinitely diversified with itself, alone takes place. And if the material world seems to be impoverished by being thus reduced to a dead mechanism, the mental is thereby enriched. All that can find no home in nature must be ascribed to the mind.

Having thus shown that the only qualities of bodies that are clearly and distinctly known in perception are extension, figure, and motion, Descartes proceeds to ask whether these qualities are known by sense or by thought. Since ' imagination ' may be taken as a general name for the whole sense-side of our nature, the question runs: Is the real essence of the piece of wax known through imagination or through pure thought ? Is it sufficient that I imagine (that is, image or picture) the wax

now as round, now as square, and now as triangular ?
Certainly not, says Descartes, for " I cannot by my
imagination run through the infinite number of
possible shapes the wax may take on, and consequently the essence of the wax cannot be realised,
compassed, adequately expressed, through the imagination." Only in conception, not in an image, nor
in a series of images, can it be known. So, too,
with the attribute of extension. Since the piece of
wax can (under the influence of heat and cold)
increase or decrease in size in an infinite number of
degrees, we do not apprehend its essence according
to the truth, if we do not think it as capable
of receiving more varieties of figure and extension
than we can ever imagine in a series of particular
images. By the understanding alone can the real
essence of a material body be known. " The perception is neither an act of sight, of touch, nor
of imagination, and never was either of these, though
it might formerly seem so, but is simply an intuition
(*inspectio*) of the mind, which may be imperfect and
confused, as it formerly was, or very clear and
distinct, as it is at present,"[1] when the attention
has separated off what is clearly and distinctly

[1] *Médit*. II. Veitch's trans. p. 112.

conceived in it, from what is obscurely and confusedly *felt*.

In the sixth *Meditation* Descartes develops further his distinction between imagination and pure conception. First he shows that they are quite distinct from one another. So long as we keep to such simple figures as the triangle, it is hard to distinguish between the conception and the image. The radical distinction between them at once appears, however, when we pass to more complex figures. If we wish to think of a chiliogon, though we cannot picture the thousand sides as we can picture the three sides of a triangle, we can yet, Descartes asserts, *conceive* the chiliogon just as easily as we can conceive the triangle. That is to say, the more complex the figure the more indistinct becomes the image, while, on the other hand, the conception remains just as clear and distinct as ever.[1]   In order that this be possible, the conception and the image must be quite distinct from one another. If they were one and the same, or essentially

---

[1] Gassendi's criticism of this argument is very much to the point (II. p. 212). All that it establishes, he there points out, is that we can comprehend in a more or less adequate manner the meaning of the *word* chiliogon, but not that we can conceive the *figure* any better than we can image it.

connected, necessarily the confusion of the image would bring confusion into the conception.

Further, in the case of complex figures, it becomes obvious that it is through the conception alone that we can have knowledge. The indistinct image whereby we represent to ourselves a chiliogon differs not at all from the image whereby we represent to ourselves a myriogon or any other figure of a great many sides, and can, therefore, be of no use for discovering the properties which distinguish a chiliogon from all other polygons.[1] And that is equally true, though not so obvious, even in the case of the simplest figures. The image even of a square is always inexact, and can therefore only be used in so far as we have compared it with the conception as its standard, correcting in it what is false and supplementing in it what is incomplete.[2] The conception is all the while the true object of the mind, and the image is really only of use as an

[1] Here Descartes' false view of geometrical science as derived from pure conceptions instead of from their construction in perception, and therefore, in image, is again leading him astray.

[2] That, however, it will be noted, does not prove that the conception has any meaning *apart from* the concrete material that it thus organises. In denying the existence of such 'pure,' that is, abstract conceptions, Berkeley is altogether in the right.

external aid in fixing and rendering more vivid the conception.[1]

Having thus shown that imagination and conception are separate and distinct from one another, and that imagination is quite unessential to adequate knowledge of the objects with which the mind deals, Descartes proceeds to prove that the essence of the mind consists in pure thought apart from all sense and imagination.[2] In the proof he applies the same method of argument as he has applied to determine

[1] Cf. above, note to p. 45.

[2] We need not be afraid to interpret quite literally Descartes' strange utterances as to the nature of imagination. He is much too emphatic on the point to allow of our regarding them as metaphorical merely. There are, he tells us, no brain-processes corresponding to pure intellection, whereas save through brain-processes imagination is not possible. *In order to form images the mind,* he further adds, *has to look outside itself at the images formed on the pineal gland* (and it must be borne in mind that Descartes believed that in visual perception there are not only two images impressed on the surface of the brain exactly corresponding to the images impressed on the two retinae but also a single image, combining them, on the pineal gland). This, according to Descartes, is the reason of the effort involved in imagining complex figures, an effort that is not required for the conception of them, conception being a process natural to the spiritual nature of the mind, and wholly immanent. Cf. *Médit.* VI. (I. pp. 323-5), Veitch's trans. pp. 151-3 ; Descartes' *Reply to Gassendi* (II. p. 297) ; *Reg.* XII. (XI. pp. 265-6). Descartes obviously here retains much of the curious scholastic doctrine of the subtilisation of material into mental images. Descartes, however, could

the essence of matter. In the soul are the three cognitive faculties, thought, sense, and imagination. These together constitute its nature, and through them does it exist. But of these only one is inseparable from it, namely, thought or conception. Since we have a clear and distinct conception of the soul apart from sense and imagination, neither can belong to its essence. Pure thought is the one attribute of mind as extension is the one attribute of body. But while thought can thus be conceived apart from sense and imagination, sense and imagination, as both involving some form of intellection, cannot be conceived apart from it. Sense and imagination are, therefore, related to thought in the same way that figure and motion are related to extension, that is, as modes to their common attribute.[1] In this way Descartes completes the

not help seeing that the above view applied only to figure, and that resistance, colour, sound, and the other secondary qualities, bear no resemblance to their physiological causes ; and hence, in treating of the physiological conditions of these sensations, he inevitably developed the more consistent occasionalistic view. Cf. *Le Monde*, chap. I.

[1] Strictly, the different conceptions or ideas are for Descartes the only proper modes of thought, corresponding to figures as the proper modifications of extension ; while sense and imagination, together with the feelings and emotions, constitute the external modifications of thought, corresponding to the motion that is externally introduced into matter.

absoluteness of his dualism.   On the one hand there exists a material world whose whole nature consists in extension and in extension alone.   On the other there exists a spiritual world whose whole essence consists in pure thought, and in that alone.   Each stands sharply outlined over against the other, and they have nothing whatsoever in common.

C¹—DESCARTES' VIEW OF TIME AND OF FINITE EXISTENCE IN TIME.

DESCARTES' view of time rests on the scholastic distinction between time and eternity.   " To be eternal is to possess entirely, perfectly, and all at once, all the attributes and perfections that the thing called eternal can possess."[2]   Since God is absolutely perfect, and also absolutely simple, His perfection can neither be added to nor subtracted from without total destruction.   All His qualities are essential qualities, and can in no way be modified by accidents that may be one moment real and another moment unreal, and so give rise to temporal succession in the mode of his existence.   Finite things, on the other hand, are so

---

[1] To p. 73, above.

[2] That is the definition given by De la Forge, following Boethius.   Cf. *Traité de l'Esprit de l'Homme*, chap. XII. p. 178.

imperfect that they are unable to possess at one and the same time all the attributes, modes, and accidents, of which their nature is capable. A material body cannot be at one and the same time round and square, at rest and in motion; the mind cannot by a single act of thought perceive all the things that it is capable of knowing. Whereas created things can be conceived through the three modes of time, *fuisse, esse, fore*, the first and last of which involves the notion of not-being; to God, the absolutely real (*maxime ens, sive ens simpliciter*), is ascribable only *esse, esse sine mutatione*.[1]

Now since God, the absolutely real, cannot be conceived save as being, He must contain in Himself the ground of His own being, and so be *Causa Sui*. Finite things, which are as easily conceived non-existent as existent, do not contain in their conception the ground of their existence, and must therefore be brought into existence by something else. That something else cannot be another finite thing, which as finite cannot create itself, and therefore *a fortiori* cannot create anything distinct from itself. The ground must therefore be God, the sole *Causa Sui*.[2]

---

[1] Cf. Clauberg : *Exercitationes*, XXXIII.

[2] Cf. *Réponses aux Premières Objections*, I. pp. 382-3.

That argument is strengthened by appeal to the scholastic principle, which Descartes employs in the proof of God's existence, viz. that it is more difficult to create substance than any of the attributes of substance. But while it was there argued that as the self has not given to itself all the perfections with which it is acquainted, it cannot have given to itself its existence, it is now urged[1] that as many of the qualities and states of the self are beyond our power to create, it is absurd to hold that the self can create that of which these are only the modes. And what holds of the self's first existence holds likewise of its continued existence. Since there are many states of the self that the self is unable to maintain, still less can it have the power to conserve that of which they are the states.

Descartes himself adds the further argument,[2] that as the self which is nothing but a thinking thing, and therefore necessarily conscious of all its activities, is unaware of actively preserving itself in existence, it cannot really do so. Since we cannot act with-

---

[1] Cf. Regis : *Cours Entier : la Metaph.* liv. I. pt. I. chap. XII Clauberg : *Exercitationes,* XXIV.

[2] *Réponses aux Premières Objections,* I. p. 383.

out being conscious that we act, absence of consciousness proves absence of activity. To the objection that neither are we conscious of the activity whereby God preserves us, Clauberg (following Clerselier) gives the reply,[1] that what is not, when it is being created for the first time, cannot feel the act creating it at the moment of creation, since it is not yet, and when it has been created, and so is able to perceive it, already God has ceased from the work of creation. The same holds true of preservation in existence, since it is due, as Clauberg consistently argues, to such separate and distinct acts of creation repeated in the separate and successive moments of time.

Since Descartes' assertion that the parts of time are independent of one another really rests, though he nowhere explicitly says so, on the assumption that time is discrete,[2] such argument defeats itself by its own internal self-contradictoriness. As the moments of time in which God recreates us are separate and distinct, either they must be indivisible, and so having no duration be incapable of composing

[1] *Exercitationes*, XXVII.

[2] Regis, it is significant, speaks of time as divisible into a *great* number of parts. *Loc. cit.*

time, or self-continuance in existence, however short that continuance be, is admitted. To recognise, on the other hand, the infinite divisibility of time is to recognise its continuity, and therefore to deny that assumption of independent *real* parts upon which the argument proceeds. This assumption of the discreteness of time Descartes partly conceals by speaking of God as *continually* conserving us. If his view of time be correct, our existence is like a line composed of dots, a repeated alternation between the state of being and the state of not-being.

This whole line of argument is of value only as an illustration of the impossible demands of Descartes' rationalism, and of the absolute occasionalism which is its only refuge. By conceiving God through the unanalysed, and mystically formed, conceptions of absolute perfection (that includes the perfection of self-caused reality), and of perfect simplicity (that does not exclude the richest variety), Descartes assumes all that is required to account for what he has made unaccountable in the finite.

D[1]—THE CARTESIAN VIEWS OF CONSCIOUSNESS.

THE two views of consciousness, which we have traced in Descartes, by commingling gave rise to a third view of great importance in the Cartesian development, the view, namely, that consciousness is no mere general name for the varying states of consciousness, but that it includes in its essence all ideas, particular ideas being but limitations or modes of it. This view, which is an excellent illustration of the Cartesian tendency to hypostasise abstract and empty conceptions into absolute realities, first appears in De la Forge, and was developed by Spinoza. "Just as every particular body has necessarily during every moment of its existence some figure that limits its extension, in the same manner the mind has always some idea that is present to it, and terminates its thought; and just as extension in general is indivisible, body in general being inseparable from any of the parts that it contains one and all at every moment within itself, and that cannot be removed outside it, and as no bounds or limits can be assigned to its extension, so likewise the thought of the sovereign and infinite Mind cannot

[1] To p. 92, above.

be divided by any particular idea; and as it is without bounds and without limits, it has no need of being terminated by any of those forms; but it includes in one single and identical thought all that can be known: so that those who deny that the mind of man has always some particular idea that limits its consciousness and determines it, unwittingly render it in a manner infinite."[1] This view of consciousness corresponds to Descartes' view of extension as the reality of the material world, at once including all bodies, and yet at the same time being quite indifferent to any particular form of body.

These conceptions, however, of extension and of consciousness, which the Cartesians would fain make the richest, are in reality the emptiest in content. If bare extension is the reality of the material world, all figure and motion are illusion; and if consciousness in general is the whole essence of mind such consciousness is the consciousness only of being in general. "At the very time when we believe that we are thinking of nothing, we are necessarily full of the vague and general idea of being . . . *this idea of being, great, vast,*

---

[1] De la Forge: *Traité de l'Esprit de l'Homme*, chap. x. pp. 128-9.

real and positive though it be, is so familiar to us and affects us so little . . . that we judge it to have little reality, and to be formed by the confused assemblage of particular ideas, although *in reality it is in it alone and by it alone that we perceive all particular existences.*" [1] Certainly, as Malebranche here asserts, consciousness of being in general is *logically* prior to the consciousness of particular kinds of being; but consciousness of being in general is in the above quotation from De la Forge, and still more explicitly in Spinoza, regarded as an absolute reality that forms the whole essence and content of particular concrete states of consciousness. Berkeley was the first clearly to demonstrate the unreality of such general notions. Being in general (and the same holds of extension in general and of consciousness in general) is, he shows, no more capable of existence than is colour in general.

A fourth view of thought, as a faculty capable of creating ideas, also appears in De la Forge,[2] as well as in Arnauld,[3] and had some ground in several of Descartes' inconsistent utterances. Spite of his proof of the passivity of mind in knowing, he asserts [4] that

---

[1] Malebranche : *Recherche*, liv. III. pt. II. chap. VIII. p. 419.

[2] *Traité*, pp. 137-8.

[3] Cf. Appendix *A*, pp. 115-6.

[4] *Réponses aux Troisièmes Objections*, I. pp. 492-3.

it possesses the faculty of producing ideas.   And again he says in one of his letters: "I have never either written or believed that the mind has need of innate ('natural') ideas, which are anything different from its faculty of thinking."[1]   Descartes' frequently quoted statement,[2] that ideas are innate in mind in the same ense that generosity or some disease is innate in certain families, is as unenlightening as it is indefinite.

[1] *Lett.* x. p. 94.   [2] *Lett.* x. *loc. cit.*

CHAPTER IV.

THE CARTESIAN PRINCIPLES IN SPINOZA AND LEIBNIZ.

In his fundamental conception of the real Spinoza completely transcends the atomistic conceptualism of Descartes. The infinite he throughout insists (developing the important line of thought that is no more than suggested in Descartes' *Meditations*) is prior both in idea and in existence to the finite. Finite beings are not independent substances, constituted by private and peculiar qualities, but as manifestations of a common substance are inwardly related. Their interaction is not the incomprehensible passing over of influence from one self-centred being to another, but the result of their mutual participation in the universal nature of things. The aim of Spinoza's philosophy is, therefore, to show how all things live and move and have their being in the all-comprehensive reality, that may indifferently be named either God or Nature.　At one time he speaks with the tongue of the religious devotee to whom God is all in all;[1] and at another in the language of science teaches the inexorable universality of natural law.[2]

The finite, which is thus neither self-explanatory nor self-active, cannot, Spinoza further insists, be explained through general or abstract notions.　"It is above everything necessary for us to deduce all our ideas from things physical or from real entities, by advancing as strictly as possible according to the sequence of causes from one real entity to another real entity, and not passing over to abstracts and universals, neither for the sake of deducing anything real from them, nor of deducing them from anything real, for in either way we interrupt the true progress of the intellect."[3] Even Descartes has been guilty of attempting to explain real phenomena from general notions.　The power of will which he ascribes both to God and to

[1] Cf. *Ethica*, v. prop. 36.　The love which we bear towards God is part of that very love whereby God loves Himself.

[2] Spinoza denies what is ordinarily understood by the freedom of the will.　Both man and God act from the necessity of their nature.　Hence also Spinoza's denial of all final causes and of miracles.

[3] *Tractatus de Intellectus Emendatione* : Van Vloten and Land's edition, ɪ. p. 33 (Stirling's trans. p. 55).

man, being a purely occult quality, is, like all occult
qualities, a mere general notion or entity of the
reason. " Will differs from this or that particular
volition in the same way as whiteness differs from
this or that white object, or humanity from this or
that man. It is, therefore, as impossible to conceive
that will is the cause of this or that volition, as to
conceive that humanity is the cause of Peter and
Paul." [1] " Man thinks himself free because he is

---

[1] *Epistula* 2. Cf. *Ethica*, ii. 48, *Scholium* (White and Stirling's
trans. pp. 94-5) : "In the same manner it is demonstrated that
in the mind there exists no absolute faculty of understanding,
desiring, loving, etc. These and the like faculties, therefore, are
either altogether fictitious, or else are nothing but metaphysical
or universal entities, which we are in the habit of forming from
individual cases. The intellect and will, therefore, are related to
this or that idea or volition as rockiness is related to this or
that rock, or as man is related to Peter or Paul." Spinoza also
gives a very complete criticism (*Ethica*, ii. 49, *Scholium*) of
Descartes' attempt (cf. above, chap iii. note to p. 110) to combine
a passive process of thinking with unlimited power of will.
There is no such thing, Spinoza points out, as a general faculty
of will, which is the source of all particular affirmations. Such
a will is an hypostatised abstraction. Affirmations differ just as
greatly as do the various ideas affirmed. Secondly, even granting that a general faculty represents anything real, there are as
good grounds for believing that we possess an infinite faculty of
perception, as there are for Descartes' contention that we possess
an infinite will. " For as by the same faculty of will we can
affirm an infinite number of things (one after the other, for we
cannot affirm an infinite number of things at once) so also by the

conscious of his wishes and appetites, whilst at the
same time he is ignorant of the causes by which he
is led to wish and desire, not dreaming what they
are." [1]   A similar criticism must be passed when men
take refuge in that other sanctuary of ignorance, final
causes and the will of God.   " When men behold the
structure of the human body, they are amazed ; and
because they are ignorant of the causes of such art,
they conclude that the body was made not by
mechanical but by a supernatural and divine art,
and has been formed in such a way so that the one
part may not injure the other." [2]   In this opposition to
general notions, Spinoza even goes so far as to deny all

same faculty of feeling we can feel or perceive (one after another)
an infinite number of bodies." And thirdly, Spinoza, in agreement with many of the best modern logicians, denies Descartes'
distinction between conceiving and judging. We have no free
power of suspending our judgment. Suspension of judgment is
itself an act of perception or judgment. " For when we say
that a person suspends judgment, we only say in other words
that he sees that he does not perceive the thing adequately.
The suspension of the judgment, therefore, is in truth a perception and not free will."

[1] *Ethica*, I. Appendix (White and Stirling's trans. p. 39).

[2] *Loc. cit.* pp. 42-3. Cf. in the same Appendix, p. 41 : "This
opinion alone would have been sufficient to keep the human race
in darkness to all eternity, if mathematics, which does not deal
with ends, but with the essences and properties of forms, had
not placed before us another rule of truth." Cf. Descartes,
Regulae ad Directionem Ingenii, IV.

objective validity to the moral and aesthetic categories. In using the general term ' man,' we leave out of sight the differences between individuals, and therefore wrongly assume that those individuals who have the same outward appearance are equally capable ot attaining the highest perfection possible for the genus ; and according as their actions are in agreement or at variance with such perfection, declare them to be good or bad.   " But as God does not know things abstractly, or through such general definitions, and as things have no more reality than the divine understanding and power bestows upon them," [1] it follows that all such conceptions, good and bad, beautiful and ugly, perfect and imperfect, are but modes of thinking, and have no application to real things.   Since each individual acts according to the necessity of his nature, it is as absurd to blame an individual for any of his actions as to condemn a triangle for not having the properties of a circle.[2]

There is, however, a curious conflict of tendencies

---

[1] *Epistula* 19.

[2] Spinoza was, of course, also forced to this position by the exigencies of his pantheism.   As all things are in God, and therefore all things divine, evil must be mere privation.   Similarly such freedom as Descartes ascribes to the individual is not only inconceivable in itself, but also incompatible with the supremacy of God.

in Spinoza's philosophy. Though he maintains that we must view things in the concrete setting of their constitutive relations, he was yet himself driven to deny the existence of the finite, the knowledge of which he thus sought to complete; and though he denounces any attempt to explain the concrete through the general and abstract, he himself in the end hypostatises, as the sole reality, a few merely abstract conceptions. The cause of this strange contradiction between the results at which he aims and the conclusions which he establishes, lies, we shall try to show, in those rationalistic principles which he shares with Descartes. The mathematical method is, he believes, the sole possible method and of universal application. " I shall therefore pursue the same method in considering the nature and strength of the affects and the power of the mind over them which I pursued in our previous discussion of God and the mind, and I shall consider human actions and appetites just as if I were considering lines, planes, or bodies." [1] And since he interprets this method in the same mistaken manner as Descartes, he likewise believes that from a pure conception (such as is unfolded in the definition of a geometrical figure, and

[1] *Ethica*, III. Preface (White and Stirling's trans. p. 105).

such as he would distinguish sharply from merely general or abstract notions) further knowledge can be directly derived. An adequate conception or definition is such " that all the properties of the thing, when the definition is considered by itself alone and not conjoined with others, may be inferred from it, as we observe is the case with the definition of a circle." [1] From ultimate conceptions, by pure deduction, all true knowledge is derived. If we can now show that this Cartesian method is at variance with the views which Spinoza seeks to maintain, we shall afford further proof of the correctness of our interpretation of that method, and also at the same time bring out more clearly its implications and consequences.

One consequence, inevitably resulting from the mathematical method, is the identification of a causation with explanation. If all things follow from their grounds in the same way that the different properties of a triangle follow from its definition, the one possible form of connection between real existences must be that of logical dependence. And that all-important consequence (implied though not openly recognised in Descartes' system) Spinoza states in the most explicit manner. Like Leibniz, he takes the principle of

[1] *Tractatus de Intellectus Emendatione* (Stirling's trans. p. 53).

causality as being a necessary truth of reason, and as identical with the principle of ground and consequent.[1] The effect is that which can be deduced with logical necessity from the notion of the cause. When no such necessary conceptual relation exists between phenomena, they cannot be causally related.[2]

This view of causation comes out clearly in Spinoza's own statement of his method in the unfinished *Tractatus de Intellectus Emendatione*. Method, he there tells us, is knowledge arising from reflection (*cognitio reflexiva*), or the idea of an idea: it is the knowledge of an idea in the mind as being true, and hence as being an instrument whereby we can acquire other true ideas. It is with the idea as it is with the reality corresponding to the idea. As all things in nature are connected with other things, their ideas will necessarily have the same connections. If anything is a cause, the effect as arising out of the cause will be deducible from the idea of the cause, and arise out of it. *Ordo et connexio idearum idem est ac ordo et connexio rerum.*

---

[1] Considered in the manner of Spinoza, it in the end resolves itself into the law of identity, the effect being one of the qualities constituting the substance of the cause. Cf. below, pp. 146-8.

[2] Cf. *Ethica*, I. 3 ; also *Epistula* 4.

But from the fact that every idea must altogether agree with the reality which it represents, " it is clear that in order that our mind may exactly reproduce the pattern of Nature it must draw all its ideas from that idea which reproduces the origin and fountain of the whole of Nature, so that it may also become the source of other ideas." [1] That primary idea is the idea of God. *Ex nihilo nihil fit*, that from which reality is to be deduced must contain within itself all that is developed out of it. We must, if knowledge of the finite is to be possible, " have a knowledge of God equal to that which we have of a triangle." [2]

Now though it be undeniable that that from which all knowledge is deducible must be the idea of an all-comprehensive Being, to affirm that is very different from saying that we must, as Spinoza implies, start straight away with an adequate idea of God, and in it by analysis discover all else.[3]   Spinoza's position

[1] *Tractatus de Intellectus Emendatione* : Van Vloten and Land, I. p. 14 (Stirling's trans. pp. 20-1).

[2] *De Intellectus Emendatione* : Van Vloten and Land, I. p. 27 (Stirling's trans. p. 44). Cf. *Epistula* 56.

[3] That is all that deduction can mean for Spinoza. The deduced is discovered to constitute that from which it 'follows.' Cf. *De Intellectus Emendatione* : Van Vloten and Land, I. p. 31 (Stirling's trans. pp. 51-2). " For in truth the knowledge of the effect is nothing else than the acquisition of a more perfect knowledge of the cause."

involves him in a dilemma.   Only if we start with
the idea of an absolute all-containing reality, can we
deduce all reality from it; yet, on the other hand, if
we start with it, we have it already, and need not to
proceed further.[1]   Spinoza, like Descartes, is here
confusing the two meanings of the term ultimate.   It
may mean that upon which all else depends, that in
and through which other things are alone conceivable,
or it may signify that which contains within itself all
else, not merely the condition but also the conditioned.
As a matter of fact, Spinoza, in the same way as
Descartes, starts from certain abstract conceptions
(these include extension and consciousness, which
Spinoza does not, and cannot, deduce from his idea
of God), and explains away all that cannot be reduced
to them.

That this perpetual interchange of the simple with
the most complex, to which all Cartesian thinking
seems condemned, should thus in Spinoza find its
most pronounced expression, is in great part due to

[1] This dilemma would not apply all-round. It applies to
Spinoza in so far as he believes that we start in knowledge from
conceptions that are known clearly and adequately, and that
from them by logical ' deduction' we derive all else. As we
have seen in considering the method of Descartes, nothing can
be derived from a conception that has not been thought in it
from the start.

the consistency with which he develops the consequences of the Cartesian interchange of real cause and
logical ground. The relation of cause and effect, he in
the end shows, is not only identical with that of
ground and consequent, but also with that of substance
and quality.[1] Since the cause is that in whose notion
the effect is necessarily and timelessly involved, the
effect must be an inherent and permanent quality of
the substance that is its ground.[2] The 'simple,' from

[1] Spinoza explicitly adopts the Cartesian doctrine that everything is either a substance or the quality of a substance.
Ethica, I. 6 coroll. Cf. *Epistula* 4 : " Besides substances and
accidents, nothing exists really or externally to the intellect."
Though the term 'accident' is here used in a very general
sense, we can still assert of Spinoza's philosophy as a whole that
it leaves no place for the conception of relations between substances relatively independent.

[2] One point, therefore, at which a critic might attack the
closely-woven web of argument that forms the metaphysics of
Spinoza is this identification of cause, reason, and substance.
The criticism would then be the criticism of Hume, that a cause
is never a reason, and an effect never a quality of its cause.
Since the fundamental fact at the root of all causal connection
is change, even if the cause be regarded as itself being or
becoming the effect, the phenomenon is still a process in time,
and therefore something which the relation of logical dependence cannot completely express. Even though it were granted
(cf. Bosanquet's discussion of the relation of cause and reason,
Logic, I. pp. 264 ff.) that ultimately the causal relation may
merge in that of ground and consequent, that would not justify
us in directly equating them, as in all forms identical. Spinoza
shows that change takes place only within a system that itself

which we start, must comprehend as its constitutive qualities all the complexity that is 'deduced' from it.

From this view of causation follows with equal inevitableness, and for the same reasons, the pantheism of Spinoza. Creation, conceived as a form of transient action, whereby God might bring into existence a reality that lay outside the circle of His own essence, is as inconceivable as any form of transient action between independent finite existences. As an effect is always an inherent quality of its cause, all causation without exception is immanent causation, and the created world the revelation of the Divine Being whose essence it constitutes.

From Spinoza's view of causation follows likewise his theory of the attributes. Since neither extension nor thought involves the other in its conception, there can be no causal relation between them.[1] Motion can produce nothing but motion, and an idea can give rise to nothing but other ideas. As both attributes, how-

is unchanging, but as the finite and changing is related to the completed system through its changing relations to other finite elements, the causal interaction of finite existences is one that still requires its own special analysis. Only when the difficulties raised by Hume's analysis of causation have been taken into account can any genuine reconciliation of causation with explanation be brought about.

[1] Cf. *Ethica*, I. 3.

ever, necessarily inhere in God, and follow from the absolute unity of His nature, they must in Him find the ground of their connection. And the only way which Spinoza can see of reconciling their absolute diversity with God's unity is by regarding each as co-extensive with the whole essence of God, expressing it in its own way. Since substance is that which exists, and is intelligible, in and through itself, it will then follow that each attribute that expresses it must be so likewise. Each will be found to obey laws that follow solely from its own essential nature. But though only these two attributes of extension and thought are known to us, God as infinitely real expresses His nature through an infinite number of such infinite attributes. And as every finite being, so far as it has real existence, shares in the essence of God, it also must be expressed through all the infinite attributes of God, and therefore, in our experience, through both the attributes of extension and of thought. That is the ground of Spinoza's fundamental principle, *ordo et connexio idearum idem est ac ordo et connexio rerum.*

Spinoza thus adopts and extends Descartes' ideal of physical explanation. Everything material, however complex or highly organised, is brought into existence through the operation of universal mechanical laws.

Mind can neither act on matter nor govern it. " When men say that this or that action of the body springs from the mind, which has command over the body, they do not know what they say, and they do nothing but confess with pretentious words that they know nothing about the cause of the action, and see nothing in it to wonder at." [1] To the objection that it is impossible that solely from the laws of the material world we should be able to deduce the causes of pictures or other works of art, and that the human body is not capable, unless it is determined and led by the mind, of building a single temple, Spinoza replies : " I have shown that [those who make this objection] do not know what the body can do, nor what can be deduced from the consideration of its nature alone, and that they find that many things are done merely by the laws of nature which they would never have believed to be possible without the direction of the mind. . . . I adduce also here the structure itself of the human body, which so greatly surpasses in work-manship all those things which are constructed by human art." [2]

[1] *Ethica*, III. 2, *Scholium* (White and Stirling's trans. p. 109).

[2] *Loc. cit.* (p. 110). As we have seen, Spinoza denies that matter is organised according to ideas which lie outside it

This ideal of scientific explanation Spinoza also applies to mind. Since mind and matter are two different expressions of one and the same reality, and run parallel to one another throughout all existence, the mind is as much a part of nature as the human body. If the human body is determined to be what it is by its relation to all other bodies in infinite space, the complex organisation of ideas which forms the human soul must similarly be determined by its relation to the other infinitely varied ideas that constitute the infinite attribute of thought. Spinoza's theory of mind is, however, less developed than his theory of matter, and constantly he fills up the gaps in his knowledge of the mental by analogies taken from the material world.[1]

in the mind of God. It is interesting to compare Spinoza's position with that of Hume. Cf. below, chap. vi. pp. 235 ff.

[1] Cf. above, Appendix *D* to chapter iii. pp. 133-5. As has been pointed out in that Appendix, the view of particular ideas as modes arising by limitation of universal consciousness is formed on the analogy of the relation of geometrical figures to the space in which they are constructed. Cf. also below, note 1 to p. 152. Spinoza retains Descartes' view of understanding as a special faculty quite distinct from imagination. Imagination is, on Spinoza's view, associative thinking, and involves a more or less explicit mental atomism. Just as he makes no attempt to reconcile his assumption of mechanical action with his theory of causation, so likewise he ignores the problem of reconciling his view of association with his doctrine of pure thought.

Now there is involved in this mechanical explanation of body and of mind that other kind of causality
in which the effect follows in time upon the cause.
One body is assumed to be able to move another
through impact, and one idea to be capable of
recalling another associated with it in the past.[1]
How such causation is possible, and in what it consists, or how it stands to the relation of logical consequence, Spinoza tells us absolutely nothing.   Yet, even
though Spinoza had clearly recognised that this form
of relation is distinct from that of logical dependence,
and had admitted his incapacity to give any definite
account of its nature, he would not, for that reason, have
been forced, like Descartes, to deny its possibility.[2]
Finite existences being, on his view, manifestations
of a single substance, transient action ceases to be

[1] Spinoza simply takes over from ordinary experience the fact
that bodies are set in motion on impact, and that ideas recall one
another.   The laws of motion he regards as necessary truths of
reason, and the laws of association he interprets (and it is an
illustration of his tendency to fill up gaps in our knowledge of
the mental by analogies taken from the material) as the subjective counterpart of the objective connections between brain
processes.

[2] That, as we have seen in the preceding chapter, Descartes is
forced to do when he consistently develops his fundamental
principles.   The occasionalist solution is the attempt to introduce in an external form that necessary relation to the infinite,
which ought to have been kept in view from the start.

inconceivable. As has already been said, it need no longer be regarded as the mysterious passing over of influence from one self-centred being to another, but rather as a natural consequence of their mutual participation in the common nature of things. Descartes' difficulty reappears, however, in Spinoza's system in a new form. As Spinoza starts from the assumption of a single substance, of which all finite existences are but modes, his problem is not so much to explain their interaction as to account for their independence. And it is in his failure to vindicate their independence, that those rationalistic principles which he shares with Descartes again reveal their inherent insufficiency.

Though Spinoza's position, as formulated in his method, is that from the conception of God, known as adequately as we know a triangle, all else is deducible, he really makes his start from the two attributes, as revealed in experience, of extension and thought. But even from these two conceptions he does not directly develop out the variety of the real. Instead of that progressive course to which his method commits him, he starts from the actual nature of finite existences, and by a regressive process, wherein the qualities constituting their finitude are explained as purely negative, reduces their essential reality to the continuous nature of extension and of thought. As regards the material world Spinoza carries out this process of reduction by first of all regarding motion as merely change of place, and therefore as purely geometrical. The sole differences in nature are differences of position and of figure. Figure, again, arises by limiting off from infinite space one finite portion of it; and as this limitation is mere negation, the finite figure *quâ* finite is unreal.[1] In extension, viewed 'concretely,'[2] no divisions or distinctions can be asserted to exist. Similarly all particular ideas are unreal limitations of universal consciousness,[3] and therefore in their finitude have no more than a negative existence. Finite existences are illusions of the imagination that vanish when their essence is realised to be continuous with, and indivisible from, the one reality. This tendency to explain finite existences, not through their

[1] Cf. *Epistula* 50: "He who says that he perceives figure, says only that he has before his mind a limited thing, and the manner in which it is limited. But this limitation does not pertain to a thing in its '*esse*,' but contrariwise in its '*non-esse*' [*i.e.* it signifies, not that some positive quality belongs to the thing, but that something is wanting to it]. Since, then, figure is but limitation, and limitation is but negation, we cannot say that figure is anything." We give Dr. Caird's translation of the passage (*Essays*, p. 354).

[2] Cf. *Ethica*, I. 15, *Scholium*: also *Epistula* 12.

[3] Cf. above, Appendix *D* to chapter III. pp. 133-5.

relations to other finite beings within an organised
system, but directly as modifications of an unchanging
reality, finds very definite expression in the *Tractatus
de Intellectus Emendatione* in a passage which we have
already partially quoted.[1]   After saying that "it is
above everything necessary for us to deduce all our
ideas from things physical or from real entities, by
advancing as strictly as possible according to the
sequence of causes from one real entity to another
real entity, and not passing over to abstracts and
universals," Spinoza adds: " It is to be observed,
however, that I do not here understand by the
sequence of causes and real entities the sequence of
individual mutable things, but the sequence only
of things fixed and eternal." And he proceeds :
" Moreover, it is not necessary that we should understand the sequence [of individual mutable things],
since the essences of individual mutable things are
not to be drawn from their sequence or order of
existence, for this gives us nothing but external
marks, relations, or at the best, unessential properties,
all of which are far from being the internal essence
of things."[2]   That last sentence is specially significant.   Spite of Spinoza's emphatic adoption of the

[1] Cf. above, p. 138.   [2] Stirling's trans. pp. 55-6.

point of view of physical science, and of his extension
of it to the mental, his thinking is still ruled by the
Cartesian opposition between internal and external,
between the unchanging essence of things and their
contingent changing relations. He fails to adapt the
timeless relation of necessary consequence, which is his
sole conception of causal connection, so as to account
for these 'external' relations. All determination, he
is forced to conclude, is mere negation, and hence can
cause nothing. There is no transient action between
finite existences, since finite existences there are none.
Differing from Descartes only in the more consistent
development of his rationalism, Spinoza equally fails to
account for the facts of our time-experience.

These results, however, as we have already stated,
by no means express the point of view which Spinoza
seeks to establish. To represent adequately the
meaning and significance of his teaching, we must also
recognise the alternative view of God, and of the
attributes, which it presents. When he develops the
above view, finite existence and change in time are
regarded as illusions, and so far as they are
explained at all, even as illusions, are accounted for
by a ghostly remnant of the spiritualism of Descartes.
They are unrealities pictured by the mind, so far as the

mind is individual, and therefore itself unreal.[1]   To
a certain extent also, the understanding is made to
account for the attributes, or rather to reconcile the
variety of the attributes with the simplicity of God's
nature.   " By attribute, I mean that which the
intellect perceives as constituting the essence of
substance."   Thereby Spinoza would at times seem to
imply that the understanding is the prism that breaks
up the white light of the Divine Substance into the
variety of its appearances.   But with that view
Spinoza is not altogether in earnest.   So soon as the
problem of reconciling the unity of God with the
variety of the attributes falls into the background, he
brings forward his alternative view of God as containing in the fullness of His being all possible reality, and
declares that the defect in our knowledge lies not in
our apprehending His unity through two wholly diverse
attributes, but in our knowing only these two, and not
an infinite number of others equally diverse.   There
is, however, no analogy possible between our knowledge of such a God and our knowledge of a triangle.

As regards the two attributes of extension and

---

[1] Spinoza, like Leibniz, declares sense to be confused thought.
All the secondary qualities would presumably, on his view,
cease to exist for perfected knowledge.

thought, a similar duality of view appears in Spinoza's teaching. When he applies his geometrical method, extension, we have seen, is regarded as simple, excluding motion and figure. Since all determination is negation, on adequate knowledge differences of figure vanish, leaving only continuous and empty space. And, in that same way, the uniform light of consciousness is regarded as known completely in any and every act of thought. When, on the other hand, Spinoza seeks to maintain the concrete reality of God, he denies that extension is the passive extension, or thought the passive thinking of Descartes. Motion is not added from outside to a passive extension, nor are the ideas, that give variety to the uniform light of consciousness, external to the nature of consciousness. Since both attributes are expressions of the Divine Substance, they reveal its inexhaustible creative energy by unceasingly giving rise, through the divine power that is in them, to all possible bodies and to all possible ideas. " From the supreme power of God, or from His infinite nature, infinite things in infinite ways, that is to say, all things, have necessarily flowed, or continually follow by the same necessity, in the same way as it follows from the nature of a triangle, from eternity and to eternity, that its three angles are equal to two right angles. The omnipotence of God has therefore been actual from eternity, and in the same actuality will remain to eternity."[1] Though this view of extension as involving motion is not developed by Spinoza,[2] and though the relation of the particular ideas to their attribute is also left quite obscure, in both cases he dwells upon the active nature of the modal existence. Each body is a *conatus quo unaquaeque res in suo esse perseverare conatur*. Similarly, each idea is regarded as having an independent existence. Containing its essence within itself, it is neither a shadowy image of an external reality nor a mere state of a mind or subject.

---

[1] *Ethica*, I. 17, *Scholium* (White and Stirling's trans. pp. 20-1).

[2] When Tschirnhausen (*Epistulae* 80 and 82) demanded of Spinoza how from the conception of extension there can be deduced *a priori* the existence of bodies that possess figure and motion, Spinoza replied (*Epistula* 83): "As to your question, whether the variety of existing things can be demonstrated *a priori* from the mere conception of extension, I think I have already sufficiently shown that that is impossible, and that, therefore, matter is ill-defined by Descartes as consisting in extension. It must necessarily be explained by an attribute which expresses an eternal and infinite essence. But this I shall, perhaps, some day, if my life be prolonged, discuss more clearly with you. For hitherto I have not been able to set down anything orderly on this matter." The above (written 15th July, 1676) is, however, the last letter which we possess from Spinoza's hand.

It is an activity expressive of the divine nature, and as such involves an affirmation.[1]

There are thus two interpretations in Spinoza of God and the attributes—a concrete interpretation in which he adopts the scientific point of view and anticipates modern thought, and the abstract interpretation to which he is forced by the inadequacy of the rationalistic principles which he inherits from Descartes.

We may now proceed to indicate, with equal brevity, the influence exercised by the Cartesian principles upon the thinking of Leibniz.[2] Like Malebranche, he holds that from the conception of the

---

[1] Cf. *Ethica*, II. 43, *Scholium*: II. 49, *Scholium*.

[2] Though Leibniz is certainly a systematic thinker, it is his many-sided suggestiveness that has been most remarked. Our aim, however, is merely to show that his system is in its main outlines based upon Cartesian principles, and that in his philosophy these principles, so far as they remain in essentials unmodified, inevitably lead to the same unsatisfactory conclusions. While, therefore, we must omit all detailed reference to those other parts of his teaching which are not closely bound up with these principles, this omission must not be taken as implying any desire, on our part, to minimise their significance and importance.

self all its different states must be capable of direct
deduction.   That, however, is not, as in Malebranche,
a final consequence to which his thinking leads, but
the fundamental doctrine upon which his system is
based.   Quite unafraid of any apparent paradoxes in
his contention, he maintains that from the idea of the
self must be deducible not only its different possible
experiences—a capacity for the different sensations
and feelings—but also the reason of the actual happening of every single 'contingent' experience, past
present, and to come.   "The nature of an individual
substance, or complete being, is to have a notion so
completed that it suffices to comprehend, and to render
deducible from it all the predicates of the subject to
which this notion is attributed. . . .   God, seeing the
individual notion or hecceity of Alexander, sees in it
at the same time the foundation and the reason of all
the predicates which can truly be attributed to him, as
e.g. whether he would conquer Darius and Porus, even
to knowing *a priori* (and not by experience) whether
he died a natural death or by poison, which we can
only know by history."[1]   This position of Leibniz is

[1] Gerhardt, ii. p. 433 (Russell's trans. p. 214).   Cf. iv. p. 436.
"The notion of an individual substance involves once for all
everything that can ever happen to it, and in considering this
notion, we can see all that can be truly predicated of it, just as

based on the atomic conceptualism, which, as we have seen, results from the scholastic doctrine of essence. Every true predicate must be included, implicitly if not explicitly, in the notion of the subject, since otherwise to assert that it belongs to the subject would necessarily be false.   Even predicates that affirm relations hold true only if they express some attribute inhering in each of the substances so related, the essence of the proposition consisting in the assertion of that inherent quality.

But if everything that can happen to an individual is included in its notion, and follows necessarily from it, if " our thoughts are the consequences of the nature of our soul, and come to birth in virtue of its notion, it is useless to demand in explanation of their appearance the influence of another particular substance, besides that this influence is absolutely inexplicable." [1]   Each soul must be a world apart. All our perceptions and feelings would arise in order as they do now, even though the whole external world were annihilated, and only God and the self remained.[2]

we can see in the nature of the circle all the properties that can be deduced from it."

[1] Gerhardt, ii. p. 69.

[2] Cf. Gerhardt, iv. p. 440.

Now just as Spinoza argues that only from the one all-comprehensive idea can the real be deduced, so Leibniz is forced to conclude that if everything is deducible from the notion of the individual, that notion must be all-inclusive.[1] Since, as experience shows, everything is bound up with everything else, and varies with it, every individual having some relation, direct or indirect, to every other individual, the above theory of predication can only be maintained through the counter-assertion that each concrete and completed notion is infinite, and mirrors in its complexity the whole Universe. Further, in order that the so-called external and accidental relations to other individuals similarly complete in themselves, be deducible from even this infinite notion, there is required, as the objective counterpart of the above assumption, the hypothesis of concomitance or pre-established harmony, the hypothesis, namely, that to every experience in one soul there must exist a corresponding experience in every other. And combining that last hypothesis

[1] Thus common to both Spinoza and Leibniz is the view of substance as that which is conceived in and through itself. But while Spinoza starts from the idea of Divine Substance to deduce the finite individual, Leibniz starts with the conception of the individual to reconstruct the Universe.

with the truth that no two individuals can be altogether alike without being identical, we may finally conclude that while each individual mirrors the same universe, each must mirror it from a different point of view. " Thus the universe is in a manner multiplied as many times as there are substances, and the glory of God is at the same time redoubled by as many representations, all different, of His work." [1] These conclusions may, Leibniz repeatedly states, appear paradoxes; but as they follow necessarily from the indubitable principle

[1] Gerhardt, IV. p. 434. Leibniz adds that each substance imitates according to its nature the infinite wisdom and omnipotence of God. " It expresses, although confusedly, all that happens in the universe, past, present, and to come, that which has some resemblance to an infinite perception or knowledge ; and as all the other substances express it in their turn and accommodate themselves to it, it may be said that it extends its power over all the others in imitation of the omnipotence of the Creator." That last sentence indicates Leibniz's mode of explaining, and justifying, the ordinary notions of causal interaction. Since the different monads mirror one and the same universe with different degrees of distinctness, change of state may well find its explanation, not in the monad in which it occurs, but in some other. One thing may be said to act in so far as it has perfection, and to be acted upon in so far as it is imperfect. And one created thing is more perfect than another when, having more distinct perceptions, there is found in it that which serves to explain *a priori* what takes place in the other. Causation is thus always ideal ; it is identical with explanation. Cf. Spinoza, *Ethica*, III. 3 ; v. 40.

that every true predicate inheres in the notion of
the subject, they must be accepted by all those
who desire to think consistently.[1]

What specially concerns us is to determine more
exactly Leibniz's meaning in the assertion that all
predicates follow from, are *a priori* consequences of,
the notion of their subject.   In seeking the relation
of predicates to their subject, two points of view
are, according to Leibniz, possible.   If we consider
the direct relation of the predicates to the subject,
the principle of their connection must be that of
identity.   The predicates follow from, are conse-

---

[1] Our attention was first drawn by the late Professor Adamson
to those letters of Leibniz to Arnauld in which the above
argument is stated.   The importance of this argument has,
however, recently been pointed out by Mr. Russell.   Mr. Russell
(*The Philosophy of Leibniz*, p. 8) holds that this argument " is
alone capable of explaining why Leibniz held that substances do
not interact."   Leibniz denies interaction because it is wholly
inconsistent with the rationalistic principles which he shares
with Descartes.   Leibniz's argument that the existence of the
composite (as it appears in ordinary consciousness) necessitates
the assumption of simple elements as its constituents—which is
the argument upon which he chiefly relies in his later works for
proof of the existence of monads—is by no means satisfactory,
since the composite is what, on his principles, cannot be
accounted for.   Cf. *La Monadologie*, sec. 2 (Latta's trans. p.
217): " And there must be simple substances, since there are
compounds ; for a compound is nothing but a collection or
aggregatum of simple things."

quences of, the notion of the subject, in the sense that by analysis they can be discovered in it, and be found to constitute it. Were anyone of the predicates changed, the subject, whose notion they express, would cease to be the same individual. In those cases, however, in which we fail to discover the predicate in our notion of the subject, we are forced to adopt a second point of view, namely, to consider the predicates in relation to the other predicates, either coexisting or preceding, and in that indirect way to determine their relation to their common subject. Though these other predicates may not involve it in their notion, and so justify it by the law of identity, they may yet supply a sufficient reason why it should be so, rather than otherwise. The problem which the philosophy of Leibniz sets to the commentator is to connect these two points of view, to reconcile the purely logical attitude expressed in the law of identity with the more empirical expressed in the law of sufficient reason. The universal application of the first would destroy both time and space, and allow only of eternal and logical, never of temporal or causal, connections. The application of the second on the other hand, implies the existence of space and time, and allows, as having at least phenomenal, practical, validity, explanation by efficient causes. From the point of view of the first, monads are notions with an eternal and completed content. From the point of view of the second, each is an activity that progressively realises its notion in time through its tendency towards the good. This opposition is identical with the opposition, which we have considered at length in our treatment of Descartes, between rational connection and temporal causation.

Leibniz, following Descartes, combines his peculiar rationalism with an equally extreme spiritualism. While an analysis of what is involved in true predication leads to the assumption of individual, completed, and all-comprehensive, notions, it is only in inner experience, Leibniz believes, that such individuality is to be found. In the *Cogito*, and there alone, do we find a unity such as those notions, if real, must possess.[1] Combining, therefore, these

[1] In it we have experience of a unity that is capable of maintaining itself throughout the variety of its states, and of an activity that progressively unfolds that unity in the realisation of desire. Further, within the unity of each perception there is always involved a multiplicity, infinitely complex. In thus insisting that in mind the two opposites, unity and variety, are inseparable, and that all *reality*—as distinguished from the unreal abstractions of thought—has that twofold aspect,

two truths, that of general reasoning and that of inner experience, Leibniz constructs a system that, however different in detail from the philosophy of Descartes, still maintains unchanged its fundamental principles.   When his rationalism comes short, active spirit is made to fill the gaps.

Leibniz does not prove that spirit has the capacity of infinite inner development.   Having shown that the notion of the individual must be all-comprehensive, and that spirit is the only form of unity in variety known to us in the real, he at once identifies the two.   In the logical

Leibniz, like Spinoza, prepared the way for a truer and more organic point of view.   The impossibility of explaining the unity of consciousness in any mechanical fashion is strongly insisted upon by Leibniz.   Cf. *La Monadologie*, sec. 17 (Latta's trans. pp. 227-8) : "It must be confessed that *perception* and that which depends upon it are *inexplicable on mechanical grounds*, that is to say, by means of figures and notions.   And, supposing there were a machine so constructed as to think, feel, and have perception, it might be conceived as increased in size, while keeping the same proportions, so that one might go into it as into a mill.   That being so, we should, on examining its interior, find only parts which work one upon another, and never anything by which to explain a perception.   Thus it is in a simple substance, and not in a compound or in a machine, that perception must be sought for."   That the spiritualism and the rationalism are very externally conjoined in Leibniz's system is not surprising, since at bottom, as interpreted by Leibniz, they are utterly at variance with one another.

notion are involved all its predicates : in the self must therefore be contained the complete conditions of all that it realises through its activities. The relation of the predicates to the subject is logical : from the self all actions must be similarly deducible. From this point, however, in Leibniz's argument the spiritualism takes the upper hand. His rationalism affords the basal argument for his monadism, but the monad being further interpreted as spirit, his rationalism is in the resulting system greatly modified to suit this deeper and more adequate conception of the nature of the individual. Since he now declares all substances to be active entities, endowed with desire and with perception, he no longer conceives the process by which the various predicates are deduced from the notion of each individual as purely, and entirely, logical. Though he still speaks of the process as *a priori*, the *a priori* reasons are such as incline without necessitating. As the development of the conscious being is ruled by the contingent principle that what is sought is the good, each of its activities is to be deduced (in accordance with that principle which inclines without necessitating) from the individual's prior knowledge of what is for the best. But in order to maintain his rationalism, even in that highly modified form, Leibniz has to make good the extreme assertions that all change in nature is the outcome of desire, and that nothing has absolute reality save subjective experience.

From his spiritualism Leibniz derives what little metaphysical explanation he is able to give of the mechanical world in space. Accepting as an empirical fact that bodies do appear to us as interrelated in space, he asserts that this appearance has its source in the confused perceptions of the monads. Thus condemning the mechanical world as phenomenal, he escapes the demand that his theory of causation be tested by the peculiar facts which it reveals. Since the mechanical world would resolve for complete knowledge into purely ideal relations between spiritual monads,[1] knowledge of it as appearance can only proceed according to the contingent laws of its actual nature. These, as experience shows, are the laws of motion. All change in

[1] Leibniz indirectly proves that the atomistic conceptualism of Descartes is as incapable of accounting for space, as, on Descartes' own showing, it is of accounting for time. The essentially relational nature of space and time, as revealed in their continuity, is inconsistent with any interpretation of reality that is exclusively based on the conception of substance.

the material world arises upon impact, and the sufficient reason for any change is therefore to be found in a preceding change capable, according to the laws of motion, óf bringing it about. But just as Leibniz fails to explain how the obscurity and confusion in the perceptions of monads should transform the discrete harmony of the universe into the continuous form of space,[1] so he fails to connect in any real way the laws of motion (which must in the end be regarded as the phenomenal manifestation of the inner striving of the monads) with the choice of the good.[2]

As regards the problem of knowledge, Leibniz's contribution is very suggestive, and in many respects anticipates modern views,[3] but when interpreted

[1] Cf. below, pp. 34-6.

[2] Cf. Russell : *The Philosophy of Leibniz*, p. 89 : " Leibniz has acquired much credit for the vaunted interconnection of his views in these two departments [Dynamics and Metaphysics], and few seem to have perceived how false his boast really is. As a matter of fact, the want of connection is, I think, quite one of the weakest points in his system."

[3] Such anticipations of more modern views are for the most part due to the principle of continuity which Leibniz applies with great acuteness and originality in all departments of knowledge. It leads him, in his theory of knowledge, to deny the absoluteness of such distinctions as those between the conscious and the unconscious, between thought and sense, between the necessary and the contingent.

quite strictly, in the light of his fundamental principles, proves less important than at first sight appears. Though he rejects Descartes' impossible opposition of thought and sense, he does so only in order to support the equally extreme contention that sense is confused thought. On complete knowledge, colour, sound, and the other secondary qualities, would, he believes, become transformed into something fundamentally different from themselves. Thinking, if it could be thoroughly carried out, would consist in a progressive elimination of sense by clarification of the confused perceptions into the distinct ideas of which they are composed. By that view of sense he seeks to mediate between Descartes and Locke, asserting with the one that the mind possesses innate ideas, and with the other that all knowledge is based on concrete sense-experience, and develops from it.

Three different views of the innateness of knowledge can be detected in Leibniz. First, there is that view which has always gone along with subjective idealism, namely, that the self is an independent substantial agent, and by reflection on its own nature acquires those notions through which it interprets all else. Since we are, so to speak, innate to ourselves, in apprehending the self we necessarily apprehend those ideas which are implied in the idea of the self, such as being, substance, unity, sameness, activity, perception.[1] This theory, however, seems to be propounded by Leibniz simply as a step towards the second and deeper view which he develops at length in the *Nouveaux Essais* in opposition to the teaching of Locke. The necessary truths of reason are not, and cannot be, guaranteed by generalisation or induction from particular instances supplied in sense-experience. They have their source in the understanding alone, and do not require for their establishment anything beyond the intelligible ideas between which they hold.[2] But since Leibniz's

---

[1] Cf. *Nouveaux Essais*, liv. II. chap. I. sec. 2 : Gerhardt, v. pp. 100-1 : "*Nihil est in intellectu, quod non fuerit in sensu, excipe : nisi ipse intellectus.* Now the soul contains being, substance, unity, identity, cause, perception, reasoning, and many other notions, which the senses cannot give." Leibniz here practically asserts that all those ideas which Locke ascribes to reflection are innate. Such reflection extends, however, on Leibniz's view, not only to the operations of the mind, but also to the mind itself. This is a view of innate ideas which Kant overthrows, one of the most important results of his philosophy being that we know objects directly, and the self only indirectly through objective experience.

[2] Though Locke cannot possibly, from his sensationalistic principles, account for such necessary intuitive knowledge, he shows himself in the fourth book of the *Essay* quite ready to

174   THE CARTESIAN PHILOSOPHY

argument, that these necessary truths are therefore
innate, implies, as he himself admits, that the ideas
between which they hold are likewise innate, his interpretation of the innateness of knowledge depends
upon his mode of regarding ideas.

Now Leibniz retains the Cartesian view of ideas as
mental existences, the objects and not the acts of
thought. "If the idea were the *form* of thought, it
would spring up and cease with the actual thoughts
which correspond to it; but being the *object*, it must
be before and after the thoughts."[1]   Each idea,
further, is to be regarded as in itself perfectly distinct.
Since experience is confused perception, and the confused presupposes distinct elements as its constituents,
all our sense-perceptions must be composed of distinct,
prior-existing, that is to say, innate, ideas.[2]   Hence,
though Leibniz himself suggests, as we shall see im-

accept Leibniz's contention that necessary truths carry their
proof in themselves, and are not formed like general truths by
induction from experience.   Cf. below, chap. v. pp. 15 ff.

[1] *Nouveaux Essais*, liv. II. chap. I. sec. 1 : Gerhardt, v. p. 99.
Cf. IV. p. 451.   As Mr. Russell (*The Philosophy of Leibniz*, p.
165) expresses Leibniz's view.   "An idea, though it is in the
mind, is neither knowledge nor desire ; it is not a thought, but
what a thought thinks about."   The above references are given
by Mr. Russell.

[2] Cf. Boutroux in his preface to the *Nouveaux Essais*, p. 94
(Paris, 1886).

mediately, a still higher and truer view of the nature of the innate ideas, he is in the end forced by his principles to adopt a view that is in essentials identical with that of Descartes. " In every soul there exist from all eternity the distinct ideas of all things. . . . The sum of these ideas constitutes reason which, in this way, is innate in us." [1]

When Leibniz is thus strictly interpreted, his most important advance upon Descartes consists in the introduction of the fruitful conception of the unconscious. Descartes had never faced the difficulty, how if, as he asserts, the essence of mind consists in self-consciousness, there can yet be innate in it ideas of which it is not at every moment conscious. It is this

---

[1] Boutroux, *ibid.* p. 82. As Leibniz thus retains Descartes' view of ideas as the objects, not the acts, of thought, the doctrine of representative perception also remains an integral part of his system. Indeed, it fits in perfectly with his view of the self as an isolated monad, reproducing in picture within itself an independently existing world. Yet while thus retaining the doctrine, he was not concerned to discuss either its grounds or its implications. Though he refers to Berkeley's philosophy as an absurd paradox, he has himself no better reason to offer for his own belief in an external world than the general principle that since being is preferable to not-being, the more existence there is the better. (Cf. Spinoza, *Ethica*, i. Appendix, at the end.) Spinoza takes up, as regards the nature of ideas and their relation to the real, a position so peculiarly his own that we have considered it needless for us to enter upon it.

unsolved difficulty which gives Locke's objections to his teaching what little force they may have.[1]   By the assumption of unconscious mental states Leibniz meets these objections, and again mediates between Descartes and Locke.

But though Leibniz thus usually ascribes independent existence to the different innate ideas, and regards them, in a mechanical fashion, as constituting the mind, there is also suggested in the *Nouveaux Essais* a third view, one that approximates more closely to the Kantian position.   For occasionally Leibniz speaks of the ideas, not as separate entities, but as " habitudes and dispositions " of the mind.[2]   " The general principles enter into our thoughts, of which they are the soul and organising bonds (*l'âme et la liaison*). They are necessary to our thinking as muscles and tendons are for walking, though we do not think upon

[1] This is one of the problems dwelt upon by Augustine. Cf. above, chap. I. pp. 9-10. When Descartes touches on this problem, he solves it in an unsatisfactory manner by ascribing to the mind a power or faculty of producing ideas. (Cf. *Réponses aux Troisièmes Objections*, I. pp. 492-3.)   Against all such faculties Leibniz, like Spinoza, carries on a vigorous polemic. A faculty must, he insists, if it is anything real, be *continously* in action in some form and degree—*quod non agit, non existit.*

[2] Cf. Preface to the *Nouveaux Essais*, Gerhardt, v. p. 45, Latta's trans. p. 367 ; also, in the first book, chap. I. sec. 26 ; chap. III. sec. 20 ; Gerhardt, v. pp. 79, 97.

them.   The mind supports itself upon these principles at every moment." [1]   Knowledge of the concrete and contingent precedes, as Locke rightly asserts, knowledge of the universal and necessary; and yet, as Descartes holds, it is the latter which renders sense-experience possible.[2]   The mind rejects the self-contradictory, even though it has never formulated to itself the law of non-contradiction.   Principles rule and govern the mind long before it acquires definite consciousness of them.   Since Leibniz, however, believes that all necessary truths are analytic, and are justified by the law of identity, he could not really develop this Kantian theory of the innateness of the connections binding the parts of our experience to one another.   By his assertion that the predicate must always be involved in the subject, he virtually reduces the judgment to the concept; whereas Kant's teaching has the contrary effect of transforming the concept into the judgment.   The judgment is the fundamental act of mind, and being essentially an act of synthesis involves synthetic connecting principles.[3]   This higher

[1] *Nouveaux Essais*, liv. I. chap. I. sec. 20, Boutroux's text, p. 190.   This passage is omitted in Gerhardt's edition.

[2] This twofold truth Leibniz certainly states much more clearly and emphatically than does Descartes.

[3] Also when an idea is interpreted as a judgment, it can no

view of the innateness of knowledge is therefore, like so many other of Leibniz's views, a suggestion merely, and for its development would involve the rejection of those Cartesian principles with which alone we are here concerned, and upon which, as we have tried to show, his monadism is based.   Only the first two views are consistent with Leibniz's principles; and since when he develops the second view, that *all* ideas are innate, his ascription of innateness to those ideas which are implied in the idea of the self ceases to have special significance, we are justified in interpreting his doctrine in that second way as in essentials identical with the teaching of Descartes.[1]

From this theory of the innateness of knowledge Leibniz has obvious difficulty in accounting for sense-experience.   As in the explanation of our apprehension of space, he assumes that the innate ideas in coming to consciousness appear first of all in a confused form. So appearing, they give rise, he asserts, not only to space but also to the secondary qualities, through which

longer be regarded in the Cartesian manner as a separate existence, the object and not the act of mind.

[1] It depends on which of the three interpretations of Leibniz's doctrines we adopt, what value we assign to his famous reply to Locke—*nihil est in intellectu, quod non fuerit prius in sensu, nisi ipse intellectus.*   Only on the last interpretation, which is no more than suggested in Leibniz, is it an anticipation of Kant.

space is apprehended. What are the causes of this confusion in our perceptions, and in what exactly it consists, Leibniz does not, however, satisfactorily explain. It must be assumed, he seems to say, because only by its means can either the finitude or the variety of the monads be established.[1] If all the innate ideas came to consciousness at once, each monad would be as God, and all monads identical. Though two explanations of such confused perception are indicated in his writings, neither can be accepted. Sometimes he speaks as if the confusion were due to the finitude of the monads, but as it is it alone that constitutes their finitude, the argument assumes all that it pretends to prove. His second mode of explanation is by the assumption of ' minute' perceptions. Confused perceptions result, he says, from the massing together of perceptions that separately are too minute to affect consciousness ; the roar of the sea, for instance, is composed of the noises made by the separate waves. This explanation is, however, equally

[1] The variety of the monads is also due, according to Leibniz, to differences in their points of view. Each represents clearly that which is near at hand, and confusedly that which is distant. This difference, however, seems to depend, as Mr. Russell points out (*The Philosophy of Leibniz*, chap. x.), on the surreptitious reintroduction of that spatial relation whose validity Leibniz denies.

unsatisfactory. For though differences of intensity may be ascribed to sensations and feelings, they can hardly be ascribed to the innate ideas, all of which are intelligible.[1]

No explanation, indeed, consistent with Leibniz's principles can possibly be devised of confused perception. It is postulated by Leibniz simply as a plausible means of reconciling an inadequate theory of knowledge with the admitted facts. Just as spirit is regarded as the source of all activity and change, so likewise obscurity in its perceptions is made to account for the secondary qualities of bodies, for space, for the finitude of the monads, and for their variety. Spirit is in the system of Leibniz, as in that of Descartes, the *deus ex machina* that solves all the irresolvable difficulties caused by a rationalism that is based on the scholastic doctrine of essence. If Leibniz's spiritualism is to be maintained, it must be upon principles fundamentally different from those which he inherits from Descartes.

[1] Cf. Russell : *The Philosophy of Leibniz*, p. 159.

CHAPTER V.

THE CARTESIAN PRINCIPLES IN LOCKE.[1]

THOUGH the English development is one of growing empiricism, it remained to the end under the
predominant influence of the Cartesian philosophy;
and Locke, the first of the school, is on the whole
more rationalist than empiric. His empiricism all-
important, and alone emphasised, at the start of
the *Essay*, but dwindling in extent and in importance
as the *Essay* proceeds, is fixed by the attitude which
he takes up towards the originals of our knowledge.
They consist, he says, of sensations which as simple
are all isolated and atomic, and between which

[1] We shall treat Locke at greater length than we have treated
Spinoza and Leibniz, partly because the connection between
his philosophy and that of Descartes has been less dwelt upon
by commentators, and also because a fuller statement of his
philosophy is necessary in order to enable us to understand the
point of view adopted by Hume in his criticism of the Cartesian
principles.

therefore, no necessary relations can ever be perceived
by us.   That assertion is obviously true, so long as
we have in view the secondary qualities of bodies.
As we have found Malebranche also insisting,[1]
between the different sensations of the different
senses, and even between sensations of the same
sense, no relation can be discovered.   But it is
not at all obvious why Locke should attempt to
interpret our whole experience in the light of the
secondary qualities.[2]   Why does he ignore the
spatial and causal relations whereby our sensations
are united to one another?   They are equally
evident, and were alone emphasised in the Cartesian
philosophy from which he starts, and yet are quite
inconsistent with such a view.   Two reasons may
be suggested.   First, the influence of Bacon with
his teaching that the inductive method, starting
from the particular facts and cautiously advancing
to the more and more general, is the only fruitful
one.   Such a method was much more congenial to
the English matter-of-fact temperament of Locke
than the adventurous *a priori* mathematical method

[1] Cf. above, chap. III. p. 95.

[2] That Locke does so appears very clearly in the section in
which he defines the nature of simple ideas (II. II. 1).

of Descartes Locke's ignorance of mathematics and interest in the purely empirical sciences of medicine and politics, and also the predominantly empirical tendency of scientific study in the England of his day, would all strengthen this influence. Still more important, however, is the physiological attitude which Locke adopted in the explanation of the origin of knowledge, and which is the natural complement of a · belief in the empirical method. All knowledge, however abstract or general, must be traced back to that sense-experience which is supplied to us in the content of detached sensations coming at different moments of time through the different avenues of sense. To admit any other source of knowledge is surely, Locke held, illegitimate, unless it can be shown (and the burden of proof he not unfairly regarded as resting on his opponents) that this, the one undoubted, and sole obvious, source of experience is incapable of accounting for it. Indeed so convinced is he of the correctness of this attitude, that he applies it also in the explanation of the mind's knowledge of its own states and activities, holding that the mind's so-called ' power of reflection' is due to an *inner sense* corresponding to, and to be explained on the analogy of, the outer senses.[1] Now that physiological attitude naturally leads Locke to his atomistic view of sensations. If sensations come to us one by one, in detached moments of time, and through different senses, then each (such we may believe is the unformulated but implied reasoning) must be capable of existing and being known separately, and being thus a completed existence cannot be essentially related to any other. If that is a true interpretation of the movement of Locke's mind, he would thereby be brought to hold that what is true of the unbridgeable qualitative differences between the secondary qualities must be true of all sensations regarded as complete mental states.[2]

Locke takes directly over from Descartes his view of the world according to which particular minds exist on the one side, and an extended material world exists independently on the other, and therefore also adopts the doctrine of representative perception. For the most part he follows

[1] Cf. below, note 3 to p. 189.

[2] The conflict between Locke's attitude in the second book of the *Essay* and that which he takes up in the fourth, is due almost entirely to the fact that while he considers only the secondary qualities in formulating his theory of the materials of knowledge, in advancing to the examination of scientific knowledge in the fourth book he finds that the only existing sciences are those rendered possible by the primary qualities.

Descartes in the interpretation which he makes of that doctrine. Bringing within the mind itself the distinction between subject knowing and object known, he assumes that over against ideas there exists a mind that knows them directly in some unexplained way, the assertion that only ideas can be objects of mind being grounded in certain un-formulated assumptions of a naïve realism. Locke, however, at times seems to interpret the doctrine in another and very different way, basing it on what he takes to be a self-evident postulate, that knowledge is only possible mediately by way of ideas, or, in other words, that the mind must always have an *idea of* the object known. Now that postulate may be correct, everything depending on the meaning given to the terms used, only it cannot on any interpretation be reconciled with Locke's other and more usual view that *only* ideas are known, and that they are known as the *objects* of mind. For if the postulate be granted, we can never know any object directly, not even an idea ; and the two views combined would therefore result in the position that all knowledge is indirect and inferential, which is absurd, involving as it does an infinite regress. Some immediate knowledge must be postulated in order to make indirect representative knowledge possible. We may therefore ignore this second view, and interpret Locke solely in accordance with the first. " [Idea] being that term which, I think, serves best to stand for whatsoever is the object of the understanding when a man thinks, I have used it to express whatever is meant by phantasm, notion, species, or whatever it is which the mind can be employed about in thinking."[1] Ideas are thus given a certain independent existence, at once illuminating the mind and being illumined by it. The mind, as Malebranche says,[2] is not '*lumière illuminante*' but '*lumière illuminée*'; and that far from luminous distinction does full justice to what is carefully kept in the half-light of a conscious indefiniteness by both Descartes and Locke. Since all those occult qualities, powers, and activities, that are driven by Descartes out of the material world, have gone to harbour in this inner world of the mind, it is a region in which no precise thinking need be expected till the coming of Hume. What is alone definite in Locke is that he is no sensationa-

[1] I. I. 8.

[2] *Méditations Chrétiennes*, I. p. 15. The phrase is quoted by Malebranche from Augustine.

list, if that means one who regards the mind as consisting of its sensations. He is, like Descartes before him, and like Berkeley after him, a spiritualist in that he assumes the existence of an abiding self that observes and compares its everchanging ideas.[1]

[1] It is from this spiritualism and not from his sensationalism, that Locke gains an explanation of our consciousness of relations, including those of space and time. As there is a self behind ideas that observes them, any relations of resemblance or of sequence that hold between them must, he believed, be visible to this self, immediately they are by it set side by side and compared. As regards consciousness of space Locke is very indefinite in his utterances. Of his description of the idea of space as simple, much the same criticism must be made as was passed upon Descartes' corresponding assertion. There is an ambiguity involved. Certainly the idea of space cannot be resolved into simpler ideas ; but that does not prove space itself to be simple in the sense in which the term 'simple' is applied to the sensations of the special senses, namely that each is a completed existence and involves no complex of relations within its content. This difficulty in the way of describing the idea of space as simple is practically admitted by Locke (II. xv. 9). In both Berkeley and Hume the dependence of our knowledge of space on a self behind ideas observing them, becomes quite explicit. Such knowledge is due, they assert, to the mind's consideration of the distribution and arrangement of visual and tactual points. This explanation by reference to a self behind ideas does not, however, account so plausibly for consciousness of space as for consciousness of time. It is impossible to hold that a variety of visual or tactual points can lie within a 'simple' sensation, and equally impossible to conceive how the mind should apprehend the different coexistent simple sensations (*minima*) of sight or touch, as forming a single

In method Locke is also the disciple of Descartes, both of them seeking by an analysis of the materials at the disposal of the mind to determine the extent and limits of knowledge. There are, however, important differences in their standpoints. While Descartes seeks the simple conceptions from which all other knowledge may be deduced, Locke as an empiricist seeks to classify the simple sensations through the mechanical combination of which all complex ideas are formed. And that difference of aim explains the greater emphasis which Locke lays on the observation by the individual of his own mind and what goes on there. Whereas the conceptions which Descartes analyses are common property, and capable of definition, sensations can only be known to each individual through his immediate personal experience of them. All knowledge must start from observation of the facts to be accounted for, and in this sphere each must observe the facts for himself.[1]

continuous field. The sensationalist theory, being formulated in the light only of the secondary qualities, is as incapable as the Cartesian rationalism of accounting for the essentially relational nature of space.

[1] The same emphasis was inevitably laid upon inner observation by Malebranche when he set himself to analyse the concrete sense-experience that Descartes had very insufficiently treated.

What Locke first discovers in looking into his own mind is the truth of the *cogito ergo sum*. He does not, however, like Descartes, regard it as a self-evident truth of reason, but simply as a fact revealed and guaranteed by introspection. " Every man being conscious to himself, that he thinks, and that which his mind is applied about, whilst thinking, being the ideas that are there, it is past doubt that men have in their mind several ideas, such as are those expressed by the words ' whiteness, loudness, sweetness, motion, man, elephant, army, drunkenness,' and others."[1] And as Locke assumes that ideas imply a self that has them, the existence of the self he takes as likewise indubitable.[2]

Locke's answer to the question—how we acquire these ideas ?—is that they come into the mind from outside through two avenues, sensation and reflection. In sensation we get ideas of external sensible objects, and from reflection ideas of the mind's own operations and passions.[3] The mind

---

[1] II. I. at the beginning.   [2] Cf. IV. IX. 3.

[3] There are many ambiguities and difficulties in Locke's view of reflection. It is by no means clear whether reflection is to be taken purely as an inner sense, corresponding to outer sense, or as a kind of self-consciousness that includes both inner and

cannot create for itself a single new simple idea. All that it can do is to unite the ideas, given through these two sources, so as to form out of them complex ideas.[1]

outer experience. The first view is prominent in his treatment of simple ideas. There he is concerned to show that all our simple ideas are passively received by the mind ; and there also he seeks to get behind them, so as to give a mechanical explanation of their origin. According to this theory, just as external objects by affecting outer sense cause sensations, so too our mental operations by affecting inner sense give rise to another and independent series of impressions. What this 'inner sense' is, Locke, it need hardly be said, is no more able to explain than he is able to explain what 'outer sense' is, and how different from the mind, nor does he pretend to. On the second view, 'reflection' is identified with self-consciousness. We can surely, Locke says, reflect on what goes on in the mind, and so have knowledge of the mind's operations. To think without being conscious that we think is as impossible as that a body should be extended without having parts (II. I. 19). Thus identified with self-consciousness, reflection must be regarded as an ultimate fact, and the previous mechanical explanation as but a preliminary metaphorical expression of what is now seen to constitute the very essence of mind. And that involves, it may be noted, the giving up of the doctrine of representative perception as regards knowledge both of ideas and of the mind's operations upon them. They are known directly, and not, like material bodies, mediately by way of intervening ideas. Also, on this second view, the separation of ideas of reflection from ideas of sensation becomes impossible. Reflection is coextensive with all knowledge, revealing not only the operations of mind, but also all the ideas upon which it operates.

[1] In describing the mind as being, prior to all experience, a

Locke fails, however, to maintain that position. As an example of his failure, and also for other reasons that will appear immediately, we may consider his account of the origin of the idea of substance. It is, he says, due to the fact that we perceive sensations to exist together in clusters (an orange, for instance, consists of the different but coexistent sensations of yellowness, roundness, softness, sweetness or bitterness, etc.), and being unable to conceive how these different sensations can subsist by themselves, or in one another, "we accustom ourselves to suppose some *substratum,* wherein they do subsist, and from which they do result ; which, therefore, we call 'substance.'"[1] The idea of substance Locke thus traces back to an ultimate fact of consciousness, to a thought-necessity, which incapacitates the mind from conceiving the contents of sensation as other than qualities, as existing

tabula rasa—a metaphor which we find also in Aristotle and in Descartes : cf. Aristotle, *De Anima,* III. 4, 429*b* 30 ; Descartes, *Reg.* XII. (XI. pp. 265, 267), *Recherche de la Vérité par les lumières naturelles* (XI. p. 345)—Locke does not mean to deny that the mind has a nature of its own, and ways of acting peculiar to itself. All that he implies is that the mind (and Descartes also agrees thereto) cannot invent a single new simple idea, and therefore must be passive in the reception of all 'simple natures.'

[1] II. XXIII. 1.

otherwise than in a something else. Sensations, he practically says, are but the occasion whereupon the mind is necessitated to produce the category of substance and quality out of itself. There is here revealed the existence of an original conception that is only explicable as having been created by the mind.[1]

This analysis of the conception of substance, inconsistent though it be with his general theory of knowledge, is in itself most valuable, and frees him at least partially from the false rationalism of Descartes. If the analysis be correct, our idea of material substance is, spite of all that Descartes may assert, neither simple, nor clear and distinct. It is a complex idea, consisting of the sum of the sensible qualities belonging to it plus the obscure and con-

---

[1] That Locke also speaks of the idea of substance as consisting, in so far as it has any positive content, of the very abstract idea of 'a something' plus the empirical notion of its acting as a bearer or support, does not destroy the fact that its formation and application is traced by him to a necessity of thought. The formal necessity only gains concrete expression through, it does not originate from, such empirical notions.

The explanation which Locke derives from his spiritualism (cf. note to p. 187) of our consciousness of relations (including those of space and time) is another example of his failure to develop his sensationalistic principles. These ideas of relation are additional, as Locke himself admits (II. xxv. 1), to the ideas compared.

fused idea of the unknown substrate which is their bearer. We are as completely ignorant of what constitutes the substance of a thing as the Indian philosopher was of what the world rested on; and our explanation is no better than his tortoise,[1] if we think that by talking of a substance we have explained anything. Since the idea of substance is an idea which arises from the necessitated regress of the mind beyond any and all known qualities out into the void, we are simply concealing our ignorance by means of a word.[2]

It is the same exactly with the idea of the self. It also is a complex idea, consisting of the sum of the mental states of which alone we are conscious plus the obscure and confused idea of the unknown self that is their bearer. " He that considers how hardly sensation is, in our thoughts, reconcileable to extended

[1] II. XIII. 19. Cf. XXIII. 2.

[2] This distinction between substance and the primary qualities is the cause of much confusion in the *Essay*. If substance be unknown and unknowable, the primary qualities cannot be regarded as copying the external object. On this second view they are effects of substance acting on our minds, and, as substance is unknowable, must be entirely different from their cause. The same consequence follows from Locke's doctrine of representative perception. Inasmuch as we know only ideas, any assertion that they resemble their unknown cause must be arbitrary and dogmatic.

matter, or existence to anything that hath no extension at all, will confess that he is very far from
certainly knowing what his soul is." [1]   And this
ignorance "conceals from us, in an impenetrable
obscurity, almost the whole intellectual world; a
greater, certainly, and more beautiful world than the
material." [2]

This discovery of our ignorance, though it limits
the sphere of our knowledge, extends the bounds of
imagination, for it establishes the possibility (which
Malebranche accepted against Descartes as regards
mind [3]) of conceiving the qualities of things as unlimited in number and variety. Beyond the simple
ideas that come to us 'in this little canton, this
system of our sun,' through the 'few and narrow
inlets' of sensation and reflection, "what other
simple ideas it is possible the creatures in other
parts of the universe may have by the assistance of
senses and faculties more or perfecter than we have,
or different from ours, it is not for us to determine."
"Only this, I think, I may confidently say of it,
that the intellectual and sensible worlds are in this
perfectly alike—that that part which we see of
either of them holds no proportion with what we see

[1] IV. III. 6.   [2] IV. III. 27.   [3] Cf. above, chap. III. note 2 to p. 103.

not ; and whatsoever we can reach with our eyes or our thoughts of either of them, is but a point, almost nothing, in comparison of the rest." [1]

Here, then, is " the horizon found which sets the bounds between the enlightened and the dark parts of things." [2] Experience, like an electric spark, is the small circle of light caused by the interaction of two unknowns. Radiating out from the double but co-incident poles of the here and the now,[3] it enables us to establish the existence of a self and of a not-self, but not to discover the nature of either or their connection. This setting of the light of our knowledge against a background of darkness gives Locke's system that appearance of solidity and depth which is so markedly absent from the unreal transparencies of the Cartesian conceptualism.

How far Locke is from regarding the metaphor of impression as a sufficient explanation of the rise of sensations in the mind appears very clearly from a tract [4] which he wrote in 1693 (that is, three years after the publication of the *Essay*). If, he there says, it be demanded, what are the causes and manner

---

[1] IV. III. 23.   Cf. II. II. 3.   [2] I. I. 7.   [3] Cf. II. XV. 12.

[4] *Remarks upon some of Mr. Norris's Books, wherein he asserts P. Malebranche's Opinion of our Seeing all Things in God,* vol. x. of the 1801 edition, p. 248.

of production of ideas in the mind, " I answer, no man can tell ; for which I not only appeal to experience, which were enough, but shall add this reason, viz., because no man can give any account of any alteration made in any simple substance whatsoever ; all the alteration we can conceive, being only of the alteration of compounded substances ; and that only by a transposition of parts." Malebranche asserts that the marigold we perceive exists as a divine idea in the understanding of God, and the ignorant assert that it exists in the garden, but " either supposition, as to this matter, is all one . . . for wherein [the alteration of the mind, we call perceiving], consists, is, for aught I see, unknown to one side as well as the other." Later on in the same tract Locke seems to say that our sole certainty is that the production of sensations is in some way conditioned by our having sense-organs. The blind man has no sensations of sight. Only in what way the sense organs aid in the producing of knowledge, that we do not know.[1]

It must be noted that Locke does not base this incomprehensibility of the production of ideas in mind, as does Descartes, on a dualism between soul

[1] Cf. Locke's other tract, *An Examination of P. Malebranche's Opinion of Seeing all Things in God*, vol. IX. pp. 214-7.

and body which renders interaction inconceivable, but on the much deeper ground that all interaction is incomprehensible. " For in the communication of motion by impulse, wherein as much motion is lost to one body as is got to the other, which is the ordinariest case, we can have no other conception but of the passing of motion out of one body into another; which, I think, is as obscure and inconceivable as how our minds move or stop our bodies by thought, which we every moment find they do. . . . The communication of motion by thought, which we attribute to spirit, is as evident as that by impulse which we ascribe to body. Constant experience makes us sensible of both of these, though our narrow understandings can comprehend neither. For when the mind would look beyond those original ideas we have from sensation or reflection, and penetrate into their cause and manner of production, we find it still discovers nothing but its own shortsightedness."[1] We are tempted to ascribe the position, which Locke here takes up, largely to the influence of Malebranche, for the passage above quoted occurs immediately after a lengthy section in which Locke criticises Male-

[1] II. XXIII. 28.

branche's acute theory of the cause of cohesion of the solid parts in bodies.[1] But, at the same time, it must by no means be overlooked that Locke's departure from Descartes' purely dualistic argument is also a necessary consequence of his own doctrine of substance. Since we know not the substance either of matter or of mind, to assert (and Malebranche asserts it still more emphatically than Descartes) their absolute diversity of nature, and consequent incapability of union, is illegitimate. As Locke says in this same section, " it may be conjectured that created spirits are not totally separated from matter," or as he puts it elsewhere,[2] it is, " in respect of our notions, not much more remote from our comprehension to conceive that God can, if He pleases, superadd to matter a faculty of thinking, than that He should superadd to it another substance with a faculty of thinking." These sections

---

[1] Cf. *Recherche de la Vérité*, liv. VI. pt. II. chap. IX. Professor Fraser asserts that in these sections Locke is criticising the theory propounded by James Bernoulli. We are not aware that there is any positive evidence that Locke was acquainted with Bernoulli's *De Gravitate Aetheris*, and in any case Bernoulli in the preface to that work points out that his theory is *identical* with that stated by Malebranche in the *Recherche*. And with the *Recherche* Locke was, of course, acquainted.

[2] IV. III. 6.

are valuable, both as showing how Locke has broken with the rationalistic dualism of Descartes, and also as preparing the way for the empirical phenomenalism of Hume.[1] For the most part, however, Locke expresses himself as personally of the belief that the self is an immaterial spirit, and frequently, in his inconsistent way, he even speaks as if we had immediate certainty of the existence of such an immaterial substance.[2]

Though Locke does not point it out,[3] his analysis of the conception of substance has also a direct bearing upon Descartes' proofs of God's existence. When Descartes speaks of an absolutely perfect being, he does not use the term perfect with any definite meaning, but solely, like the term infinite, as a synonym for absoluteness. Now the *impossibility* of defining ultimate reality is what (if this analysis of the conception of substance be granted to be

[1] Cf. also in same chapter of *Essay*, section 32.

[2] Cf. in the same chapter, from which the above quotations are taken, section 15 at the end. To the objections of the materialists as to the obscurity and incomprehensibility of the notion of spirit, he has the counter-argument that as great difficulties are involved in the notion of matter. Cf. sections 31 and 32.

[3] Locke indeed refuses to express an opinion as to the validity of the ontological argument.

adequate) is here established by Locke.   Since God is thought as substance and so as absolutely real, necessarily His very conception involves existence. The absolutely real must be real—true, but altogether trivial.   The important question is as to what is the nature of absolute reality, and towards the answering of that question Descartes' proofs can yield no aid.[1] Spiritualism and materialism—such must be Locke's final conclusion—alike pretend to knowledge where none is possible.

When we turn to Locke's account of scientific knowledge in the fourth book of the *Essay*, we at once discover how overwhelmingly strong was the influence exercised upon his thinking by the rationalism of Descartes.   He holds, with Descartes, that knowledge is of two kinds, intuitive and demonstrative. We perceive intuitively that white is not black, that a circle is not a triangle, that three are more than two, and equal to one and two.   Such truths are given together with the ideas compared, and immediately on the presentation of the two ideas the mind cannot but intuitively perceive the relation between them.   " This part of knowledge is irresistible, and like bright sunshine forces itself immediately

[1] Cf. above, note to p. 58.

to be perceived as soon as ever the mind turns its view that way."[1]   Demonstrative knowledge is formed of an unbroken series of such original intuitions, whereby the mind is led on from one intuitive truth to another.   Since we cannot perceive directly the relation of equality between the three angles of a triangle and two right angles, we must "find out some other angles, to which the three angles of a triangle have an equality; and finding these equal to two right ones, come to know their equality to two right ones."[2]

But though thus adopting Descartes' views as to the nature of rational science, Locke yet considers the demand that all truth be discovered by a deductive method to be impossible of realisation.   A twofold method is necessitated by the difference between our knowledge of modes and our knowledge of substances.[3]   Take the abstract conception of a

[1] IV. II. 1.

[2] IV. II. 2.   Obviously Locke in this illustration regards mathematical knowledge as gained not from abstract conceptions, but from the construction of them in perception, the intermediate links being added as required. How this reconciles with his view of mathematical knowledge as purely conceptual, dealing with abstract ideas, it never occurred to Locke, any more than to Descartes, to inquire.

[3] Modes are those complex ideas which, however compounded, contain not in them the supposition of subsisting by them-

triangle as a figure formed by the intersection of three straight lines in space. The mind, Locke holds, needs not to call in experience, nor to go beyond the idea with which it starts, in order to discover innumerable new properties belonging to it. To the attentive mind it develops out spontaneously according to an inner logical necessity. That view of our knowledge of modes is the explanation of those statements in the *Essay* which sound so strangely in the mouth of Locke, the sensationalist. "It is the contemplation of our own abstract ideas that alone is able to afford us general knowledge."[1] "The true method of advancing knowledge is by considering our abstract ideas."[2] Quite otherwise is it with the conception of a substance, say of gold. As the simple ideas which make up this complex conception bear no relation to one another, it is barren and unproductive: the yellow colour, for instance, has nothing to do with its coldness to the touch, and no connection is visible between either

selves, but are considered as dependencies on, or affections of, substances, *e.g.* the mathematical conception 'triangle,' and the ethical conception 'gratitude.' The ideas of substances are such combinations of simple ideas as are taken to represent distinct particular things subsisting by themselves.

[1] IV. II. 16.   [2] IV. XII. 7.

of these qualities and its malleability.   Whereas the conception of the triangle is an organic conception, all its properties presupposing one another, the complex idea of gold is but a cluster of disconnected sensations.

This difference Locke further unfolds by his distinction between nominal and real essence.   While the nominal essence of a thing consists only of the sum of the external characteristics, whereby we identify it, the real essence contains the primary and fundamental qualities from which all the others result.   Now in the case of modes the nominal and the real essence are always the same.   From the conception of a triangle, as a space enclosed by three straight lines, all its other properties can be directly deduced.   As a real essence the conception is the cause and ground of each and every one of them. In exactly the same way Locke conceives substance. He did not hold as we do now that each substance is in its peculiar nature constituted by the relations in which it stands to other substances.   Influenced by that same doctrine of essence that clung, as we have seen, to the thinking of Descartes, the fundamental category through which Locke regards nature is not that of causality, but that of substance.   Locke asks, not for a cause of becoming, but for a cause of being, the unchanging ground of the unchanging nature of the thing. Each material substance is regarded as having a real essence quite as much as any mathematical construction.[1] Did we know the real essence of gold "it would be no more necessary that gold should exist, and that we should make experiments upon it than it is necessary for the knowing the properties of a triangle, that a triangle should exist in any matter; the idea in our minds would serve for the one as well as the other."[2]

[1] It is true that no one could be more emphatic than Locke himself in stating the objections to such a view. "Put a piece of gold anywhere by itself, separate from the reach and influence of all other bodies, it will immediately lose all colour and weight, and perhaps malleableness too: which, for aught I know, would be changed into a perfect friability. Water, in which to us fluidity is an essential quality, left to itself, would cease to be fluid" (IV. VI. 11). Yet these facts do not lead him to discard the view of things as separate substances each with an essence peculiar to it, but only to reinforce in his mind the hopelessness of ever getting to know the real essences upon which the purely intrinsic qualities as well as these powers of producing effects on neighbouring bodies depend. For he concludes in the immediately following paragraph: "If this be so it is not to be wondered that we have very imperfect ideas of substances; and that the real essences on which depend their properties and operations are unknown to us." Cf. III. VI. 6:—"[The real essence is] that particular constitution which everything has within itself, without any relation to anything without it."

[2] IV. VI. 11.

It is because we are ignorant of this inner essence that we are incapable of discovering the necessary connection which exists between the different sensible qualities, or of deducing from them any quality that we have not experienced to coexist with them.

The same distinction Locke expresses in yet another way, which brings out the difference in the universality of the knowledge which each yields. The idea of the triangle is not only a real essence, revealing necessary connection between its different properties, but also an archetype formed by the mind for its own use, and hence yields an unfailing test of the universality of ideal judgments. It enables us to distinguish in any concrete image between the properties that follow from the particular length of its sides and the size of its angles, and those which, as involved in, and following from, the archetype of all triangles, hold with complete universality. Of substances, on the other hand, the archetype exists without us, and is unknown, and hence in their case we can have no such criterion whereby to distinguish accidental from real connection. It is with our knowledge of substances as it would be with our mathematical knowledge, if the mind possessed only particular concrete images and not also the conception of the ideal which is but imperfectly realised in any one of them. Each proposition would hold of the particular triangle from which it was taken, but no further. In the case of substances we are reduced for increase of knowledge to induction, and to an induction that is always precarious and uncertain.

Thus, then, while in mathematical science all knowledge develops from within, from contemplation of our abstract ideas, in physical science all knowledge develops from without, through the senses. In the one our method is purely deductive; in the other purely inductive.

The criticism to be made of this position is that when Locke asks the all-important question—Wherein lies the cause of this difference between our knowledge of modes and our knowledge of substances?—he has no other answer to give than the fanciful rationalistic one, that there must be real essences in the case of substances as well as of modes, and that the discovery of these would render all knowledge equally certain and equally rational. Had Locke been able to free himself from this false rationalism, and instead of interpreting the facts through a fanciful theory, asked how *any* real essence can have this strange power of yielding new and certain knowledge, he would have found that this peculiar characteristic of our ideas of modes [1] depends on the nature of space and time, and a thorough analysis of space and time is the proof of the incompleteness of his theory of sensations as all simple and relationless. That theory is true to the facts so long as we have in view solely the unbridgeable qualitative differences between our special sensations, but it ignores, and leaves unaccounted for, the spatial and temporal connections, as well as the categories of substance and attribute, cause and effect, whereby they are all bound together in organic connection one with another. Locke's Cartesian theory of mathematical reasoning as purely conceptual and deductive is false, while his Baconian theory of physical reasoning as purely inductive is incomplete. Still, though Locke's theory of both is thus unsatisfactory, and though he misinterprets both in the light of an inherited rationalism, it is his merit that he so dwelt on the difference between them, as to force

---

[1] Locke adds moral conceptions to the number of the modes, but the discussion of that addition lies outside our inquiry.

the problem of their relation on the attention of his successors.

If we now follow him in his further analysis of our empirical knowledge we shall see how his empiricism strangely dwindles, until it almost disappears. To the question,—Can experience afford us universal propositions such as this, that ' all gold is malleable ' ?—Locke is forced to reply in the negative. All that experience shows is that in the particular bits of gold, which we examine, malleability goes along with the other properties by which we identify gold; but as it reveals no necessary connection between malleability and the other properties, it can give us no ground whatsoever for asserting that they will coexist in all other bits of gold which we may care to examine in the future. " General certainty is never to be found but in our ideas. Whenever we go to seek it elsewhere in experiment or observations without us, our knowledge goes not beyond particulars. It is the contemplation of our own abstract ideas that alone is able to afford us general knowledge." [1]

Locke's position here is open to misunderstanding. It will be objected that it is nonsense to say that

[1] *Essay*, IV. VI. 16.

it is only probable that all men will die or that
the sun will rise to-morrow. Gold always does
act in the same way, and therefore the possibility
of its not doing so in the future is not worth
attending to. But that is not the point. Locke
is not doubtful as to the practical certainty of many
generalisations from experience. The distinction,
which he wishes to make, lies not between certainty and probability, but between demonstrative
certainty and empirical certainty, the difference *in
kind* between empirical and conceptual knowledge.
In the case of connections between ideas it is impossible to conceive the opposite; the nature of
each idea related involves within itself its relation
to the other, and to change the relation would be
to change the nature of the ideas related. In
the case of matters of fact no connection can
be perceived between subject and predicate save
only that of *de facto* conjunction in our experience,
and the opposite is quite conceivable. Hence the
defect in our empirical knowledge is not that we
cannot tell whether the connection asserted will
remain the same in all future cases, but that we
can never discover by experience, however extensive,
any connection at all between them.

Yet Locke remains so much under Descartes' influence that he goes to the extreme of holding that this empirical knowledge is not entitled to the name of knowledge at all, and that sense-experience can perform no function in scientific knowledge. The only hope for natural science lies in its assimilation to mathematics by discovery of the real essences of substances. This hankering after a knowledge of the real essences of bodies comes out again and again in the *Essay*. "The essence of a triangle lies in a very little compass, consists in a very few ideas; three lines, including a space, make up that essence. . . . So I imagine it is in substances, their real essences lie in a little compass, though the properties flowing from that internal constitution are endless."[1] "In the knowledge of bodies, we must be content to glean what we can from particular experiments; since we cannot, from a discovery of their real essences, grasp at a time whole sheaves, and in bundles comprehend the nature and the properties of whole species together."[2]

Here the ambiguity in Locke's doctrine of substance, according to which at one time substance is

[1] II. XXXII. 24.
[2] IV. XII. 12. Cf. IV. VI. 11, already quoted on p. 204.

identified with the primary qualities, and at another taken as something wholly unknown behind them, is again apparent.   For the most part, throughout the fourth book of the *Essay*, substance is identified with the primary qualities, and by knowledge of the real essence of body, he means knowledge of those modifications in the primary qualities upon which the secondary qualities and powers depend. Thereby the qualitative element in experience would be subjected to the mathematical method, and all the various facts of experience could be deduced from the ultimate constitution of bodies.

But that is impossible, Locke finds, for three reasons.   First, because we do *not* know that constitution of the minute parts on which all the other qualities depend : and secondly, because even if we did, we would not be able to perceive any connection between it and the sensations which the body produces in us.   Primary and secondary qualities are not related as substance to its properties, but as cause to effect, the two being quite heterogeneous. Also, thirdly, we cannot even assert, Locke admits, that the secondary qualities do depend upon the primary : the real essence may lie deeper in " something yet more remote from our comprehension."

According to his doctrine of substance in the second book of the *Essay*, he ought to have said, not that they may, but that they do depend upon something more remote than the primary qualities. The primary qualities are themselves effects, and therefore may not at all resemble their causes.

For these three reasons, therefore, anyone of which is by itself sufficient, we cannot apply the mathematical method in natural science; and hence Locke 'suspects' that a science of nature is not possible. Falling himself into the error of Descartes, he seeks entirely to exclude the empirical element, and to make science purely rational and deductive. For Locke, as for Descartes, mathematical reasoning, falsely interpreted, remains the ideal of knowledge. Empirical knowledge when compared with this ideal is condemned in every respect.

Considering now, in conclusion, Locke's philosophy as a whole, we see how his theory of mathematical knowledge is borrowed from Descartes and incorporated practically without change into his sensationalism. He was of course forced by his sensationalistic starting-point to assert that ultimately all our mathematical conceptions are derived from experience, but how that is possible he nowhere

explains in any satisfactory way, his treatment of
space and time being among the least consistent parts
of a very inconsistent system.   Yet we are not
justified in regarding Locke's theory of mathematical
reasoning as brought externally, as an altogether
foreign element, into his system.   Good grounds can be
given for taking up exactly the opposite attitude and
regarding Locke as a rationalist, and his sensationalism
as but externally tagged on to his rationalism.   These
grounds are his spiritualistic view of mind as an
active agent combining and comparing ideas; his
belief in the absolute certainty and intuitive evidence
of mathematical truths; his use of mathematical
knowledge throughout the *Essay* as the ideal of
all scientific knowledge, and the standard whereby
empirical knowledge is condemned and found wanting;
and, lastly, his suggestion that by a conceivable, though
not practicable, extension of our knowledge (by the
discovery of the real essences of substances) our
sensations would cease to be all relationless, and would
appear as necessarily bound up one with another, and
so as capable of rational deduction from one another.
In that last position Locke shows himself to be
a more complete rationalist than even Descartes, who
despaired of the possibility of thus rationalising the

sensible. But as all that is really fruitful in Locke
is due to his empiricism, and as nearly all these
rationalistic elements are survivals weak in their
falsity, it is perhaps more charitable still to call
him a sensationalist.

CHAPTER VI.

HUME'S CRITICISM OF THE CARTESIAN PRINCIPLES.

HUME'S achievement is, we shall try to show, two-fold. In the first place, by his analysis of the causal relation he refutes the fundamental assumption involved in the Cartesian rationalism, viz., its identification of causation with explanation. And, in the second place, by his complementary analysis of mental activity he demonstrates the illusoriness of that spiritualism by which Descartes and his successors seek to conceal the radical defects in their teaching. How much of the Cartesian system remains when its spiritualism and its rationalism are thus excised, and what effect these remaining doctrines have on Hume's own thinking, we shall then decide.

We shall best lead up to Hume's criticism by first considering the position of Berkeley. Berkeley's endeavour is to reconcile the teaching of philosophers, that the only possible object of mind is an idea, with the belief of the vulgar, that the mind immediately perceives the real things. " I do not pretend to be a setter-up of new notions. My endeavours tend only to unite and place in a clearer light that truth which was before shared between the vulgar and the philosophers . . . the former being of opinion that *those things they immediately perceive are the real things*, and the latter that *the things immediately perceived are ideas which exist only in the mind.* Which two notions put together do, in effect, constitute the substance of what I advance." [1] This reconciliation Berkeley claims to have achieved by his assertion that perceived ideas are the real. Nothing exists but minds and their ideas.

That position is specially significant for us as being the outcome of a consistent development of Descartes' principles. Descartes' three fundamental principles, viz., his doctrine of representative perception, his spiritualism, and his rationalistic view of causation, all combine to compel its acceptance. An immediate consequence of the doctrine of representative per-

[1] The Third Dialogue between Hylas and Philonous : at an end.

ception, recognised by Descartes himself, is that though the whole material world were annihilated, provided sensations were still produced in our minds in the same orderly manner as now, we should never suspect that such an important event had taken place. The doctrine of representative perception detaches the mind from the material world. Though we may infer, we can never perceive its existence.

Secondly, if by a cause we mean that from which the effect can be deduced, and through which it can be rendered comprehensible, material bodies must be admitted to be as inefficacious as they are invisible. Just as they cannot be perceived, so neither can they cause perceptions. If the material world exists, it is an addition to the sum of creation that, so far as man is concerned, is altogether superfluous. It can fulfil no function that will justify its existence. It uselessly mirrors in shadowy projection, without the bright variety of sensuous appearance, what takes place quite independently in the minds of men. As incapable of ordering itself as of producing sensations, it demands continuous divine intervention for the transmission of motion, and so serves only to increase twofold the labours of God. By abolishing this superfluous material world Berkeley simplifies and develops the occasionalist theory.   As spirit is the sole conceivable cause, so also it is the sole possible form of existence ; and ideas are its states.

Like the occasionalists, Berkeley bases his system upon the principle of causality, assumed to be a self-evident truth.   That principle he interprets as meaning that every idea is produced by a will.[1]   The only intelligible causation is creation.[2]   God produces in our minds from moment to moment the various sensations that constitute for us the real world in space.   And creation out of nothing is the prerogative of finite as well as of infinite spirit.[3]   When we call up this or that idea we recreate it, painting it anew, as Locke says, upon the mind.   It is no more than a fiat of the will, and it is done.   Similarly the finite spirit is capable of creating its own desires, and upon these desires God produces new sensations in it and other minds.

From this conception of spirit Berkeley also gains an explanation of our knowledge of relations.[4]   Re-

[1] *Commonplace Book* (Fraser's edition), p. 462.

[2] Which is also the central principle of the metaphysics of Geulincx.

[3] *Commonplace Book, loc. cit.*

[4] "All relations including an act of the mind, we cannot so properly be said to have an idea, but rather a notion of the relations and habitudes between things," *Principles*, sec. 142.

cognising the very obvious fact that relations cannot exist between ideas that, following Locke, he has described as all simple and relationless, he regards them as superinduced upon the ideas by the activities of the occult mind behind them. The impossible thus being made possible, they are apprehended (though not known) through 'notions.'[1]

Berkeley's system is thus the most absolute spiritualism and occasionalism conceivable. An occult self, supposed to lie behind our ideas, observing and comparing them, is brought in to solve the difficulties arising from his atomistic sensationalism, and an infinite mind to solve all the difficulties that remain.[2]

That Berkeley took little trouble to establish the reality or to define the nature of spiritual substance need not be found surprising, since this spiritualism

---

[1] Berkeley also uses the term 'notion' to signify the consciousness, distinct from knowledge proper, through which we apprehend the self as an active agent. In this way, by what is on his principles a quite unmeaning term, he was able to keep out of sight the fact that the self is a hypothetical existence, assumed in order to account for what would otherwise be unaccountable in our experience, and that it is therefore on the same basis as material substance, requiring for its conception all those abstract notions that he has denounced as unintelligible.

[2] Just as spirit is introduced by Descartes and Leibniz to solve the difficulties of their atomistic conceptualism.

existed complete, though latent, in Descartes and
Locke.   After Berkeley's negative criticism of them,
it simply remains as his one valuable inheritance
from their philosophies.   Now, however, that it has
thus in Berkeley shown itself in its true colours, it
is clamant for the criticism of Hume.   Certainly, if
we suppose spirit to be capable from its very nature
of doing all the things demanded of it by Berkeley,
capable when infinite of creating sensations, and
when finite of creating images, the effects will be
explained, but it will be the illusory explanation by
the occult.

Just because of that false view of spirit Berkeley's
attitude towards the ' external ' world is also quite
untenable.[1]   So long as the self is regarded as a
particular finite existence, distinct from all other
selves, the bringing of reality within it is impossible,
and is really the direct opposite of the position of
ordinary consciousness.   For it is by no chance that
Berkeley calls the known objects ideas.   He may
insist that they are also the realities which all
people believe in ; they are yet ' realities ' that exist

[1] With the most valuable parts of Berkeley's teaching, viz.,
his analysis of sense-perception and development of empiricism,
we are not here concerned.

separately, numerically and existentially distinct, in the mind of each person perceiving them.[1] They are created anew by God in the mind of each observer, and pass into nothingness when that individual ceases to observe them. Also, though Berkeley insists that mind knowing and ideas known are inseparable in their antithesis, practically all the reality is given to mind. It is not the sensations that constitute the real, but infinite spirit, on the one hand, that creates them from moment to moment, and the finite spirits, on the other, in which they are thus given a momentary existence. He adopts the extreme occasionalist position. There are as many different worlds as there are minds, and the only connection between these completely isolated minds is through the external agency of a miraculously acting Deity.[2]

[1] Berkeley's frequently attempted denial of this is nothing better than a mystification of his readers. Cf. *Dialogues*, III. (Fraser's edition), I. pp. 343-4.

[2] The real problem is not whether, when ideas are conceived as the objects of mind, a second kind of objects is also necessary—in his answer to that question Berkeley may be in the right—but whether such subjective ideas have any reality. That Berkeley never thought of asking that last question is the proof that he has not been able to free himself from the physiological point of view which he attacks. For only the assumption of the truth of that point of view (cf. below, note 3 to p. 249) could

We may now pass to Hume's criticism of the Cartesian principles.   In attacking the Cartesian identification of causation with explanation, Hume throughout emphasises the time-aspect of the causal relation.[1]   As there is no necessary connection or inseparability (and this must be admitted by all) have driven his predecessors to the conclusion, which he shares with them, that knowledge is a purely subjective process in the mind of the individual.   The physiological point of view may, or may not, be an impossible one for the explanation of knowledge, but there is no question that it cannot be overthrown by arguments that tacitly assume its truth.   In a word, Berkeley's idealism can offer good grounds for itself, *if we grant the doctrine of representative perception*.   That doctrine, however, Berkeley does not prove, but assumes ; and it rests on those very grounds which Berkeley rejects.

[1] Berkeley had already denounced the Cartesian doctrine of essence, "the current opinion that everything includes within itself the cause of its properties ; or that there is in each object an inward essence which is the source whence its discernible qualities flow, and whereon they depend."   Of the existence of such substances we have no proof, and of their nature we can form no conception.   The only conceivable objects of mind are disconnected sensations, each of which (such as in an orange, the colour yellow, or the sensation sweet) is a unit complete in itself.   The separate sensations are not qualities of, but units constituting, the clusters or 'things' to which they belong. And the relation of substance and quality being thus eliminated by Berkeley, the category of causality became all-important both in his own and in Hume's system.   Berkeley also prepared the way for Hume's view of causation by his contention that sensations can never be necessary causes, but only arbitrary signs one of another.

between the idea of an event as something happening in time and the idea of a cause, Descartes' assertion that the principle of causality is a self-evident truth of reason must be categorically denied. Since what we call cause and effect are always distinct events, each of which is known separately in a single impression, they can always be thought apart without contradiction.[1] Hume's contention is implicitly recognised by those philosophers who have offered demonstrations of the principle—demonstrations which, as Hume found, are all fallacious and sophistical. Hobbes argues that as all the points of time and space, in which we can suppose any object to exist, are in themselves equal, unless there be some cause, which is peculiar to one time and to one place, and which by that means determines and fixes the existence, it must remain in eternal suspense; and can never begin to be for want of something to fix its beginning. To which argument Hume has the unanswerable reply: " Is there any more difficulty in

---

[1] We may note, in passing, that the final value of Hume's analysis of the causal relation is seriously affected by the dogmatic psychological atomism upon which it is made to rest. In describing causal connection as merely sequence, even though it be invariable sequence, he ignores—to mention only one factor—the continuity of time.

supposing the time and place to be fixed without a cause, than to suppose the existence to be determined in that manner ? . . . If the removal of a cause be intuitively absurd in the one case, it must be so in the other: and if that absurdity be not clear without a proof in the one case, it will equally require one in the other. The absurdity, then, of the one supposition can never be a proof of that of the other; since they are both upon the same footing, and must stand or fall by the same reasoning." [1]

The argument of Clarke is that if anything wanted a cause, it would produce *itself*; that is, exist before it existed; which is impossible. And in a similar fashion Locke argues that if anything is produced without a cause, it is produced by *nothing*, or, in other words, has nothing for its cause, which is absurd, since nothing can never be a cause, any more than it can be something or equal to two right angles. Now both these arguments are, Hume holds, plainly inconclusive, and, like that of Hobbes, assume the principle which they pretend to establish. " When we exclude all causes we really do exclude them, and neither suppose nothing nor the object itself to be the

[1] *Treatise*, I. III. III. pp. 381-2.

causes of the existence; and consequently can draw no argument from the absurdity of these suppositions to prove the absurdity of that exclusion." [1]

The remaining argument, that every effect must have a cause, because that is implied in the very idea of effect, is merely verbal. "Every effect necessarily presupposes a cause; effect being a relative term, of which cause is the correlative. But this does not prove that every being must be preceded by a cause; no more than it follows, because every husband must have a wife, that therefore every man must be married." [2]

The universal principle is, then, not demonstrable by reason. That the mind instinctively frames its demands in accordance with it, and that until these demands are fulfilled, the mind remains intellectually dissatisfied, Hume is not concerned to deny. [3] He maintains only that if the principle is thus neither self-evident nor demonstrable by reason, such dissatisfaction, even though inspired by the principle, cannot be regarded as proving its validity.

[1] *Treatise, loc. cit.* p. 383.   [2] *Ibid.*
[3] Hume himself traces this instinctive demand to the ultimate constitution of our human nature. Expressing only the practical demands of our human nature, it affords no knowledge of reality either within or without the limits of experience.

Reason as little avails to prove the necessity of the causal connection between particular events. Dwelling on what Malebranche, Locke, and Berkeley had already made clear, Hume shows how never in a single case can we by *a priori* reasoning discover in our idea of a cause any capacity to produce a particular effect.[1] Every effect, without exception, is a distinct event from its cause, and hence can never by reason be discovered in it.[2] But if reason here comes short, so also does sense-experience, since from it we can never extract one jot of evidence in support of our belief in necessary connection. Though that was admitted of all material processes by Locke and Berkeley, they had yet

[1] Cf. *Enquiry*, sec. IV. pt. I. pp. 25-6 : "We fancy that were we brought on a sudden into this world we could at first have inferred that one billiard ball would communicate motion to another upon impulse ; and that we needed not to have waited for the event, in order to pronounce with certainty upon it. Such is the influence of custom, that, where it is strongest, it not only covers our natural ignorance, but even conceals itself, and seems not to take place, merely because it is found in the highest degree."

[2] Here again Hume's atomistic sensationalism affects the statement of his argument. Whereas Locke had rightly limited himself to the assertion that *for us, owing to the incompleteness of our knowledge*, the connection between cause and effect is incomprehensible, Hume frequently seems to imply that the actual relation of causation consists of nothing but mere sequence, and is therefore *in itself* necessarily incomprehensible.

held that we are conscious of internal power,[1] when by the simple command of our will we move our limbs, or call up an idea. Apprehending in that way what causal agency is, we are able, they believed, to infer to it elsewhere. Now certainly the motion of our limbs follows upon the command of our will. Of that we are every moment conscious. But of the means by which it is effected, of the energy by which the will performs so extraordinary an operation, we are very far from being conscious, and must indeed admit the causal agency to be here, even more than elsewhere, unknown and inconceivable. The connection between the volition in the mind and the movement in the body, instead of being the key to all other causal connections, is what most calls for explanation. " Were we empowered by a secret wish to remove mountains or control the planets in their orbit, this extensive authority would not be more extraordinary nor more beyond our comprehension."[2]

[1] Cf. Locke's *Essay*, II. XXI. secs. 4 and 5.

[2] *Enquiry*, sec. VII. pt. I. p. 54 : Geulincx (*Ethica*, Tract I. chap. II. sec. II. § 14) similarly asserts that it is no less miraculous that upon the command of my will, when I seek to pronounce the word earth, the tongue in my mouth should tremble, than if the whole earth had thereupon trembled. Cf. Malebranche : *Méditations*, IX. pp. 111-3.

Nor can we pretend to be acquainted with any power in the soul by which it is able to produce an idea at will. That would be "a real creation, a production of something out of nothing."[1] "So far from being conscious of this energy in the will, it requires as certain experience, as that of which we are possessed, to convince us, that such extraordinary effects do ever result from a simple act of volition."[2] As Malebranche points out, such creation is not even conceivable. "I deny that my will produces in me my ideas; for I cannot even conceive how it could produce them, since my will, not being able to act or will without knowledge, presupposes my ideas and does not make them."[3] "Is there not here," Hume asks, "either in a spiritual or material substance, or both, some secret mechanism or structure of parts, upon which the effect depends, and which, being entirely unknown to us, renders the power or energy of the will equally unknown and incomprehensible?"[4] Or as Hume in accordance with his theory of association might have gone

---

[1] *Enquiry, loc. cit.* p. 56.   [2] *Enquiry, loc. cit.* p. 57.

[3] *Eclaircissement sur chap. iii. pt. ii. liv. vi. de la Recherche.* As Malebranche adds, the mind does not even 'create' its desires.

[4] *Enquiry, loc. cit.* p. 57.

on to explain, the mind produces no ideas; it is the ideas in consciousness that by virtue of their mysterious associative quality, themselves attract others into consciousness; and as this associative quality is as unknown in its workings, and as incomprehensible, as the force of gravity between material particles, we must admit that causal agency is not known in the mental any more than in the material world.

It has frequently been asserted that Hume in his theory of causation in no way advanced beyond the occasionalists, or at least not beyond Malebranche and Berkeley. The falsity of such a view is sufficiently indicated by the criticisms which Hume, in accordance with his new views, is compelled to make of the occasionalist system.[1] It is the occasionalists, he shows, who are the most flagrant of all offenders in making use of the idea of causation as if it represented something positive and conceivable. Resorting on all occasions to a creative intelligence, they use it unrestrainedly to explain anything and everything, as in its occult indefiniteness it is only too well fitted to do. They assume that we gain in immediate experience knowledge of

[1] We shall have more to say on this point. Cf. below, pp. 241-5.

the self as an active agent, and conceiving God on
the analogy of the self, they ascribe to Him all
those effects of which the self is found to be incapable. They differ among themselves only in the
division they make of power between the self and
God. Berkeley regards the self as creative with
regard to its images, God as creative in all else;
whereas Malebranche goes so far as to deny efficacy
to any of our volitions, and regards God as the
cause of our ideas, as well as of our sensations and
of the motions of our limbs. And if we try to
estimate which is the more unsatisfactory position
of the two, it is hard to decide. Malebranche has
the virtue of siding with Hume and the facts in
his denial of all creative power to the self; but
since knowledge of spirit as endowed with creative
power is only to be derived from the self, he just
thereby renders his theology the weaker.[1] Descartes
applied the principle of causality to connect the uncon-
nectable soul and body, and also to connect God with
the self and with the world. The first application of
the principle easily yielded to criticism, but it was
Hume who first saw that exactly the same criticism
holds *with still greater force* against the asserted relation

[1] Cf. below, note 2 to p. 241.

of God to the self and to the world. We only deceive ourselves when we pretend to explain anything, not to speak of everything, by a God that is a magnified projection of an occult self.

Since Hume by his analysis of that spiritualism whose influence we have traced in Malebranche, Leibniz, Locke, and Berkeley, reveals the ungrounded nature of Descartes' view of the self as a substance distinct from its experiences, and of the complementary view of God as a separate existence, the cause and creator of all else, we may proceed to consider his arguments in detail. The self is only to be found in the organised unity of its concrete experiences, and not in a substance behind them.[1]

[1] The self is not simple and indestructible, but infinitely complex and continuously changing. It is in order to emphasise against Descartes and his followers this fact of the complexity and changeableness of the self that Hume asserts that it is "nothing but a bundle or collection of different perceptions, which succeed each other with an inconceivable rapidity, and are in a perpetual flux and movement. Our eyes cannot turn in their sockets without varying our perceptions. Our thought is still more variable than our sight; and all our other senses and faculties contribute to this change, nor is there any single power of the soul, which remains unalterably the same, perhaps for one moment. The mind is a kind of theatre, where several perceptions successively make their appearance; pass, re-pass, glide away, and mingle in an infinite variety of postures and situations. There is properly no *simplicity* in it at one time,

"I cannot compare the soul more properly to anything than to a republic or commonwealth, in which
the several members are united by the reciprocal
ties of government and subordination, and give rise
to other persons, who propagate the same republic
in the incessant changes of its parts. And as the
same individual republic may not only change its
members, but also its laws and constitutions; in like
manner the same person may vary his character
and disposition, as well as his impressions and ideas,
without losing his identity. Whatever changes he
endures, his several parts are still connected by the
relation of causation.[1] And in this view our identity
with regard to the passions serves to corroborate

nor *identity* in different; whatever natural propension we have
to imagine that simplicity and identity. The comparison of the
theatre must not mislead us. They are the successive perceptions only that constitute the mind; nor have we the most
distant notion of the place, where these scenes are represented,
or of the materials of which it is composed" (*Treatise*, I. IV. VI.
pp. 534-5). Hume's analysis of the self has often been very
unfairly treated by being considered only in relation to the
later views of Kant. It ought rather to be interpreted in the
light of his opposition to the views of his predecessors and
contemporaries. When Hume's arguments are so regarded, it
must be admitted that, whatever error his own views contain,
he is altogether in the right against Descartes, and is really
working towards the position of Kant.

[1] It must be borne in mind that Hume maintains his right to
speak of events as 'causally' connected. Cf. below, pp. 242-3.

that with regard to the imagination, by the making our distant perceptions influence each other, and by giving us a present concern for our past or future pains or pleasures."[1] The theory, that ideas may be explained as the modes of a simple substance, refutes itself, as explanation by the occult always does, when more universally applied. There are, Hume points out,[2] two systems of things, the real and the ideal, that demand explanation. In the real world there exist the sun, moon, and stars; the earth, seas, plants, animals, men, ships, houses, etc. These, Spinoza asserts, must all be regarded as only modifications inhering in a simple, uncompounded, and indivisible substance.[3] Similarly, Hume proceeds, in the ideal world, viz., the universe of my mind, I observe another sun, moon, and stars, an earth, seas, towns, houses, etc.; and in short everything that I can discover or conceive in the first system. These, according to the theologians (among whom must be counted Descartes and his followers), are also modifications, and modifications of one

---

[1] *Treatise*, I. IV. VI. p. 542. [2] *Ibid.* I. IV. V. p. 525 ff.

[3] This statement, it need hardly be pointed out, is not quite fair to Spinoza. That, however, does not really affect Hume's argument. The Cartesians certainly take an abstract, not a concrete, view of the unity and simplicity of the self.

simple, uncompounded, indivisible substance. Now
is it possible to discover any absurdity in the one
hypothesis that is not common to both; and if the
Spinozistic hypothesis fails to advance our comprehension of the material a single step, must not the
same admission be made as regards the spiritualistic
interpretation of knowledge ?

If instead of calling thought a modification we
give it 'the more antient and yet more modish
name of an action' nothing whatsoever is gained
by the change. As we know only ideas, and have
no conception either of a mind that is distinct from
them, or of action in any form, to call the ideas
actions of the mind is both meaningless and useless.
Also, since the theologians cannot pretend to make
a monopoly of the word action, the 'atheists' may
"likewise take possession of it, and affirm that
plants, animals, men, etc., are nothing but particular
actions of one simple universal substance, which
exerts itself from a blind and absolute necessity.
This you'll say is utterly absurd. I own 'tis unintelligible ; but at the same time assert, according
to the principles above-explained, that 'tis impossible
to discover any absurdity in the supposition, that
all the various objects in nature are actions of one

simple substance, which absurdity will not be applicable to a like supposition concerning impressions and ideas."[1] And that being so, it goes without saying that the explanation of our knowledge of relations as due to the activity of a self that takes the different ideas out of their externality, and holding them together in its own indivisible unity observes their relations, must equally be rejected. We have no knowledge of any such abiding self behind our ideas, capable of observing them, nor can we form any conception of those activities that are here ascribed to it.

Hume further analyses the notion of mental agency in his criticism of the argument from design.[2] That argument rests, he points out, on the assumption that material bodies cannot give order and arrangement to themselves, and that in mind or reason alone is an organising principle to be found. Experience is appealed to. "Throw

---

[1] *Treatise*, I. IV. V. pp. 528-9.

[2] It is the only general proof of God's existence unnoticed by Descartes, and that for the obvious reason that it is irreconcilable with his elimination of all final causes from his physics. It became prominent in Leibniz. Spinoza's arguments against final causes are in many respects curiously analogous to those of Hume. Cf. below, chap. IV. p. 140 and pp. 149-50.

several pieces of steel together, without shape or form; they will never arrange themselves so as to compose a watch; stone, and mortar, and wood, without an architect, never erect a house. But the ideas in a human mind, we see, by an unknown, inexplicable economy, arrange themselves so as to form the plan of a watch or house. Experience, therefore, proves, that there is an original principle of order in mind, not in matter. From similar effects we infer similar causes. The adjustment of means to ends is alike in the universe as in a machine of human contrivance. The causes, therefore, must be resembling."[1] Admirable conclusion!—until we reflect. No principle of order in matter? What about the forces of attraction and repulsion, which we daily observe at work? No organising principle save mind? "In this little corner of the world alone, there are four principles, *Reason, Instinct,*

[1] *Dialogues concerning Natural Religion*, pt. II. p. 395. These dialogues have been strangely neglected by Hume's commentators. And yet they represent the maturest results of Hume's thinking. They were repeatedly elaborated by him throughout a period of twenty-seven years. "The work, penned in the full vigour of his faculties, comes to us with the sanction of his mature years, and his approval when he was within sight of the grave" (Burton's *Life of Hume*, I. p. 325).

Generation, Vegetation, which are similar to each other, and are the causes of similar effects. What a number of other principles may we naturally suppose in the immense extent, and variety of the universe, could we travel from planet to planet and from system to system, in order to examine each part of this mighty fabric?"[1] A tree bestows order and organisation on that tree, which springs from it, an animal on its offspring, a bird on its nest.

To say, Hume further urges, that this order in animals and vegetables proceeds ultimately from design, is begging the question, unless it can be proved by *a priori* arguments, that order is inseparably attached to thought, and can never of itself belong to matter. Neither of these positions can, however, be established.[2] The order into which our ideas fall ' of themselves' is no more an ultimate fact than is the organisation of an animal or plant.[3] The order in all three cases depends upon an inconceivably complex variety of causes. "Nothing seems more delicate with regard to its causes than thought. . . . A difference of age, of the

---

[1] *Dialogues,* pt. VII. pp. 422-3.   [2] *Ibid.* p. 423.

[3] Cf. *Dialogues,* pt. VIII. p. 430, quoted below in note to p. 239.

disposition of his body, of weather, of food, of company, of books, of passions; any of these particulars, or others more minute, are sufficient to alter the curious machinery of thought, and communicate to it very different movements and operations. As far as we can judge, vegetables and animal bodies are not more delicate in their motions, nor depend upon a greater variety or more curious adjustment of springs and principles."[1] And just as we have experience of order alike in mind and in matter, so have we also of disorder in both, of madness in the one, and of corruption in the other. Why then should we think that order is more essential to the one than to the other? So far as we can pretend to penetrate into the nature of mind, ideas tend to fall into order because they obey the laws of association, which correspond to the law of gravity between material particles. " But reason, in its internal fabric and structure, is really as little known to us as instinct or vegetation; and perhaps even that vague, indeterminate word, *Nature*, to which the vulgar refer everything, is not at the bottom more inexplicable."[2]

The argument from design therefore assumes

[1] *Dialogues*, pt. IV. p. 408.   [2] *Ibid*. pt. VII. p. 423.

everything in asserting that intelligence is known as a principle, and the sole principle, of order; and when that assumption is detected, it becomes obvious that to explain the world as created is merely to push the problem further back, and that it is every whit as reasonable to 'explain' the world as having been generated, or as having grown from a seed. The Creator, in order to work intelligently and with design, must first have created a plan, but in order to create that plan intelligently, he must plan it also, and so on in infinitum.[1] If it means any-

---

[1] Hume's argument is an interesting inversion of the Platonic argument, used to prove the reality of an ideal archetypal world. Cf. Norris's *Theory of the Ideal World*, pt. I. pp. 27-9 : "Tho', considering the power of its Almighty Author, [the world] was made out of *nothing*, yet, considering his wisdom, it must be made according to *something*, and he that raised this stately fabric without any praeexistent *matter*, could not yet be conceived to do it without any praeexistent *form* or *idea*. For as he could not make it without forethinking of it, so neither could he think of it without having something to terminate that thought, which must be the nature or essence of the thing that was to be made. . . . Hence the sensible must be made according to some other *prae-existent nature* that was so essentially exhibitive and representative of it, as to be after the manner of an original pattern or model of it, as having all that *intelligibly* which itself has *sensibly*, which is no other than that ideal world we are contending for." Hume here shows how this argument cuts both ways. The real cause of its failure is that we can form no conception of ideas as archetypes

thing to say that the different ideas which compose
the reason of the Supreme Being fall into order of
themselves and by their own nature, why is it not
as good sense to say that the parts of the material
world fall into order of themselves, and by their
own nature ? Can the one opinion be unintelligible
when the other is not so ? It is, of course, replied
that what produces the order in the ideas of God
"is a rational faculty, and that such is the nature
of the Deity. But why a similar answer will not
be equally satisfactory in accounting for the order
of the world, without having recourse to any such
intelligent creator, as you insist on, may be difficult
to determine. It is only to say, that *such* is the
nature of material objects, and they are all originally
possessed of a *faculty* of order and proportion.
These are only more learned and elaborate ways
of confessing our ignorance ; nor has the one

preceding reality. The order of our ideas depends on experience ;
and the assumed Creator, as there is nothing outside his mind,
can have no such experience. Cf. Hume's *Dialogues*, pt. VIII. p.
430 : " In all instances which we have ever seen, ideas are
copied from real objects, and are ectypal not archetypal, to
express myself in learned terms. You reverse this order, and
give thought the precedence. In all instances which we
have ever seen, thought has no influence over matter, except
where the matter is so conjoined with it, so as to have an equal
reciprocal influence upon it."

hypothesis any real advantage above the other, except in its greater conformity to vulgar prejudices."[1]

With Hume's destruction of the occult self, that is the ultimate source of all occult qualities, the occasionalist system of Descartes collapses like a house of cards. "I cannot perceive any force in the arguments on which this theory is founded. We are ignorant, it is true, of the manner in which bodies operate on each other: their force or energy is entirely incomprehensible. But are we not equally ignorant of the manner or force by which a mind, even the supreme mind, operates either on itself or on body?... Is it more difficult to conceive that motion may arise from impulse than that it may arise from volition? All we know is our profound ignorance in both cases."[2] A causal

---

[1] *Dialogues*, pt. IV. pp. 409-10.

[2] *Enquiry*, sec. VIII. pt. I. pp. 59-60. Cf. Malebranche, *Méditations*, IX. p. 111 : "How stupid and ridiculous are the philosophers! They imagine that creation is impossible because they cannot conceive how the power of God can be sufficiently great to create something out of nothing. But can they conceive how God is capable of stirring a straw? If they attend thereto, they will find that they cannot comprehend the one more clearly than the other, since they have no clear idea of efficacy or of power; so that if they follow out their false principle, they should conclude that God is not even sufficiently powerful to give motion to matter. But this false conclusion

explanation of things as due either to matter or to a divine infinite mind is equally illusory. We have no idea of what a sufficient cause would be like: certainly mind is as little as matter known to be the sufficient cause of anything. If, on the other hand, we are content to regard a cause merely as that which always precedes an effect, and never accounts for it, then, so far as our experience goes, only a mind that is united to a body can cause anything; and in this union matter has as much influence on mind, as mind on matter.[1] Such causal interaction of soul and body is as conclusively proved by experience as any causal connection can be, and the denial of it is an instance to what arbitrary denial of the most evident facts the pretence of comprehending causal connection will lead philosophers. Matter and motion, it is argued, however varied, are still matter and motion, and can cause nothing but change in the position and situation of bodies; it is absurd to imagine that motion of

would land them in opinions so foolish and so impious, that they would become an object of scorn and of indignation even to the most ignorant." Yet Malebranche declares God to be unknowable and incomprehensible alike in His nature and in all His ways, and so is himself in the end forced to the agnostic conclusion of Hume.

[1] Cf. *Dialogues concerning Natural Religion*, pt. VIII. p. 430.

brain particles in one direction should be a passion, and in another direction should be a moral reflection.[1] Irresistible as that argument may seem, we have only to recall the preceding reasoning to be reminded that so far as our insight goes anything may produce anything, and that though there appear no manner of connection between motion and thought, the case is the same with all other causes and effects. The connections, which Berkeley dogmatically names arbitrary, are in fact only incomprehensible. Locke was altogether in the right in asserting that incomprehensibility is no ground for denying the causal connection in either case. "This communication of motion by thought . . . is as evident as that by impulse. . . . Constant experience makes us sensible of both of these, though our narrow understandings can comprehend neither."[2]

For Descartes an effect is that which can be deduced with logical necessity from the notion of the cause. Like all the other Cartesians (and the occasionalists are not exceptions to the rule), he failed to see that since by an effect we mean that which follows *in time* upon its cause, or in other words that

[1] *Treatise*, I. IV. V. pp. 529-30.
[2] *Essay*, II. XXIII. 28. Cf. chap. on Locke, pp. 196-9.

since the principle of causality is the law of change, such logical relation cannot possibly express its nature. As the logical relation is timeless, not only is it wrong to assert that where it is not to be found causal relation must be absent, we can on the contrary affirm that where it does hold the relation cannot be that which is properly denoted by the term 'causal.'[1] The first to perceive this was Hume; and from the conclusions which he thereby established far-reaching consequences follow. If causation, which is the bond connecting the phenomena of our time-experience, cannot be rationalised, the Cartesian rationalism, and therewith its spiritualism, must fall to the ground.

An entirely new set of problems is, indeed, raised by Hume. If the principle of causality is neither self-evident nor demonstrable by reason, with what right does the mind interpret experience in the light of it ? Also if the mind can never form any conception of what would be a cause adequate to produce an effect, how can it decide in particular cases that phenomena are so related ? By the former question Hume inspired Kant in the establishment of a rationalism that, unlike the scholastic rationalism of Descartes, is reconcilable with the facts of our time-

[1] Cf. above, chap. IV. note 2, to p. 147.

experience; and by the latter question became the founder, in a much truer sense than Bacon, of the modern theory of induction. In both he transcends the rationalism of Descartes.

Hume is here, we may say, introducing into metaphysics the point of view of physical science. The Cartesian identification of causal connection with logical dependence inevitably involves its further identification with the relation of substance and quality. The effect, regarded as a logical consequence, must be a permanent quality of the substance that is its ground. And being thus dominated by the category of substance, Cartesian thinking results, as we have seen, either in an atomism or in an empty pantheism. Through Hume's analysis, however, the relative position of the two categories is inverted. Throughout modern thinking all qualities tend to be regarded as effects due to causal interaction between substances that apart from such relation are granted to be inconceivable. The centre of gravity is shifted from the separate things to the organised system in and through which they exist. This is the real meaning, or at least (thanks to Kant) the final outcome, of Hume's analysis of causation and of spirit.

So far we have merely been stating Hume's

position, and may now pass to criticism of it. He adopts Locke's view of the materials of knowledge as consisting of isolated atomic impressions ; but as he denies that we can form any conception of a self that might take such ideas out of their externality, and holding them together, thereupon perceive relations between them, he has to admit that he is incapable of accounting even for our consciousness of time. " All my hopes vanish, when I come to explain the principles, that unite our successive perceptions in our thought or consciousness. I cannot discover any theory, which gives me satisfaction on this head." [1] That admission must not, however, be taken as justifying the Cartesian view of the self. Rather we may hold that such a view of experience disproves itself in demanding as its indispensable complement the assumption of an occult self.[2] Hume's false view of

[1] This confession occurs in the Appendix to vol. III. of the original edition of the *Treatise* (I. p. 559 of the edition of Green and Grose).

[2] Though Kant was unacquainted with Hume's examination in the *Treatise* and in the *Dialogues* of the Cartesian spiritualism, he in the end developed, under the pressure of his own principles, views very similar to those of Hume. At first, however, his adoption of Hume's view of the materials of sense forced him to maintain the Cartesian view of the self as a separate existence, preceding knowledge and rendering it possible. Cf. below, chap. VII. pp. 260-2.

experience, as consisting of atomic impressions, itself results from what was the really serious limitation to his thinking, namely his retention of the fundamental Cartesian doctrine that knowledge is a purely subjective process, and that all we can ever know are our own subjective states. That that position is inconsistent with his general principles and with many of his explicit utterances, only shows how deep-rooted it was in his mind, and how completely unconscious he was of therein making assumptions. He starts off excellently. Though he retains from his predecessors the terms, impression, perception, and idea, to denote the objects known by us, they are, he insists, to be regarded as perfectly neutral terms. By 'ideas' he does not mean, like Descartes, Locke, and Berkeley, the objects or modes of mind. As we can form no conception of a mind or subject, we cannot so view them. Nor are they ideas *of* objects, for that implies that there exist ideas *and* objects, and such a duality of existence Hume demonstrates to rest on an illusion, and to be the error that gives rise to all the contradictions of the Cartesian dualism. Hence, instead of Hume's contention being that we know nothing but purely subjective states, it is rather that nothing subjective as distinguished from objective is conceivable by us. His true position, if only he had been able to maintain it, is, like that of Kant, phenomenalism, and not subjective idealism.

Such an objective view of knowledge appears in the following passage. "As every perception is distinguishable from another, and may be considered as separately existent; it evidently follows, that there is no absurdity in separating any particular perception from the mind; that is, in breaking off all its relations, with that connected mass of perceptions, which constitute a thinking being. The same reasoning affords us an answer to the second question. If the name of *perception* renders not this separation from a mind absurd and contradictory, the name of *object*, standing for the very same thing, can never render their conjunction impossible. External objects are seen, and felt, and become present to the mind; that is, they acquire such a relation to a connected heap of perceptions, as to influence them very considerably in augmenting their number by present reflections and passions, and in storing the memory with ideas. The same continued and uninterrupted Being may, therefore, be sometimes present to the mind, and sometimes absent from it, without any real or essential change in

the Being itself." [1] That view is, however, only
stated in order to be refuted, and proofs, that prove
nothing of the kind, are given to show that perceptions have no continuous existence, but are "dependent
on our organs, and the disposition of our nerves and
animal spirits." [2] "All impressions are internal and
perishing existences and appear as such." [3] "Let us

---

[1] *Treatise*, I. IV. II. pp. 495-6.   [2] *Loc. cit.* p. 498.

[3] *Loc. cit.* pp. 483-4. In Descartes and Locke, we have seen,
as before them in Augustine (cf. above, chap. I. pp. 4-5, 13-14),
the problem of knowledge is pushed further back without being
in any way solved. They adopt the physiological point of view
in the explanation of knowledge, and as a consequence of that
point of view formulate the doctrine of representative perception.
The elementary facts of physics and physiology seem to make
the assumption of the truth of that doctrine unavoidable (cf.
above, p. 116). If the mind knows by means of the brain, and
if (as these sciences prove) the brain is only stimulated indirectly
by the vibrations transmitted to it from distant objects, the
objects themselves can only be indirectly known through the
mental states they thus cause. Reasoning in this way, Descartes
and Locke feel compelled to bring the external objects within
the mind in the form of images, and to assume that it is by
looking at these mental images that it acquires knowledge of
the real objects they represent. What the nature of these
images can be, which allows of their copying material extended
bodies, and yet at the same time of their appearing in an
immaterial unextended mind, they never explain, save by
asserting that they are ideas and therefore naturally capable of
existing in mind. Similarly they as little explain what mind
is, or how it knows these mental images ; here again the description of mind, as that which knows, is supposed to suffice.

fix our attention out of ourselves as much as possible: Let us chase our imagination to the heavens, or to the utmost limits of the universe; we never really advance a step beyond ourselves, nor can conceive any kind of existence, but those perceptions, which have appeared in that narrow compass." [1]   Spite, then, of Hume's assertion to the contrary, he still holds to the Cartesian trinity of mind, ideas, and matter, and is therefore still within the Cartesian system, still at the point of view of naïve realism and physiology.   In all essentials he takes up the position of Locke, that all we can know of human nature are certain of its qualities, propensities, or instincts, and that we can never penetrate into the nature of bodies or know them otherwise than by those external properties which discover themselves to the senses.

Now it is really that belief in the subjectivity of knowledge, with the retention of the physiological

The only difficulty, however, that is removed thereby, even in appearance, is that of local difference between mind knowing and objects known. All other difficulties remain as unsolved in this dualism of mind knowing and ideas known, as they were in the previous dualism which it is assumed in order to explain, of mind knowing and external objects known. Hume, like Berkeley, in admitting the subjectivity of knowledge, assumes the truth of Descartes' dualism even while attacking it.

[1] *Treatise*, I. II. VI. p. 371.

point of view which it implies, that has prevented Hume from discarding Locke's definition of the materials of knowledge. Like Locke and Berkeley, he believes that in the distinction between the different senses he has supplied to him a means for the analysis of our concrete experience, and for the classification of its ultimate elements. The different sensations supplied to the mind one by one through the different senses constitute experience, and hence any idea that cannot be regarded as capable of transmission into the mind through one or other of these distinguishable avenues must be denied. And it is by taking Hume's own point of view (and purely physiological it undoubtedly is), that we shall most fitly reply to him. Is the brain, we may ask, that reacts upon peripheral stimuli, to count for nothing? If the single, central brain, in reacting upon stimuli, transforms them, what becomes of the supposed isolation and unrelatedness of the given sensations?

Owing to this oscillation between phenomenalism and subjective idealism, Hume's thinking frequently becomes very confused. Invariably he distinguishes between mental and physical laws, comparing association to the force of gravity, and yet obviously if perceptions alone are known, the only known 'causal' laws are those of association. Especially does confusion appear in his views as to the inter-action of soul and body. Mentally connected our sensations and our *perceptions* of our bodily states undoubtedly are, but this connection between per-ceptions Hume tacitly interprets as a connection between mental states and bodily antecedents.

Hume is thus only half-emancipated from the Cartesian system that he attacks. His conception of knowledge is still that of a process which takes place separately in each individual, and which, if perfect, would recreate the external world in picture within each individual mind. "We never really advance a step beyond ourselves, nor can conceive any kind of existence but those perceptions which have appeared in that narrow compass." So long as that fundamental tenet of the Cartesian philosophy has not been called in question, its dualism of mind and matter, of internal and external, cannot be over-thrown. It was left to Kant to explode the theory which Hume had undermined.

CHAPTER VII.

THE TRANSITION TO KANT.

KANT, like Hume,[1] regards all systems previous to his own as being either dogmatic in their principles, or else purely negative and therefore self-contradictory in their scepticism. But, Kant further adds, both schools have certain presuppositions in common, presuppositions in which Hume also shares. Dogmatists and sceptics alike believe that it is the function of knowledge to reproduce an external world in picture within each individual mind; and when they find it impossible to account for such knowledge from the nature and constitution of the external world, they either fall back on a pre-established harmony, the most shallow of all explanations in Kant's opinion, or, ignorant of their own ineradicable dogmatism, triumph in their self-caused failure. Kant was the

---

[1] *Treatise*, I. IV. I. pp. 474-5.

first to call in question this assumption, that the
function of knowledge is to reduplicate an independent reality.[1] May it not be, he asks, that the
world we construct in thought is altogether different
from the real outside us?   And if so, is it to be
condemned on that account?   May not the material
world exist only for us, and yet be a very real
world with a nature and structure of its own, which
it will be the work of our human science to determine?   That is what Kant calls his Copernican
idea.   Since the history of philosophy has demonstrated that it is impossible to make cognition
conform to objects, we must reverse the supposition,
and suppose objects to conform to our ways of
knowing.   On that hypothesis we may hope to explain better the facts of knowledge.   Locke and
Hume, as they admit the nature of the self to be
unknowable, have no right to follow Descartes in
his assertion that it is unoriginative in the production of knowledge; and immediately their naïve
realism is rejected, the opposite is seen to be the
more natural view.   If the self, in relation to which

[1] Even though Hume holds that the function of our actual
knowledge is purely practical, he still preserves, as we have
seen, the Cartesian ideal of knowledge as a subjective repro-
duction of an external world.

experience exists, has a nature of its own, it will like everything else have its own peculiar organisation and modes of activity, to which objects, if they are to be known at all, must conform. Nothing can enter into the mind, save by conforming to the laws of mind.

The complement of that new view of the nature of knowledge was a fresh theory of philosophical method. As early as 1764 we find Kant strongly condemning the mathematical method. "Nothing has been more injurious to philosophy than mathematics; that is, than the imitation of its method in a sphere where it is impossible of application."[1] While mathematics starts from conceptions (such as that of a triangle or a square), which, as arbitrarily *constructed* by the mind, are known exhaustively; philosophy deals with *given* conceptions (such as those of space, time, and spirit), that in their obscure complexity resist complete analysis.[2] Such

[1] *Untersuchung über die Deutlichkeit der Grundsätze der natürlichen Theologie und der Moral, Werke* (Hartenstein), II. p. 291.

[2] Though in mathematics a few such irresolvable conceptions (those of magnitude, unity, space, etc.) are also involved, they are presupposed by it, not its objects, and therefore do not require to be mathematically defined. It is just where mathematical definition becomes impossible, that philosophy has to begin.

conceptions are known, but known only as problems. "As Augustine has said, 'I know well what time is, but if anyone asks me, I cannot tell.'"[1] We have the conception of spirit, but whether the object of that conception is or is not distinct from matter, we cannot from the mere examination of it decide.[2] Philosophy must start from the obscurely apprehended actual, not from the conceptually necessary. Kant names his own method the 'transcendental,' which outlandish title need not conceal from us that it is simply the hypothetical method of physical science applied in the explanation of knowledge. Taking our actual knowledge as the fact to be accounted for, we must discover what are the conditions that can alone render it possible.

The most characteristic feature in Kant's treatment of knowledge has still, however, to be mentioned, namely, that he takes as the fact to be explained not experience in all its multiplicity,

[1] Quoted by Kant, *Werke*, ii. p. 292.
[2] Cf. *Träume eines Geistersehers* (1766), *Werke*, ii. pp. 327 ff. 359, 378. Much of Hume's criticism of the Cartesian spiritualism (that criticism being of course developed quite independently by Kant) is to be found in this treatise. Kant repeats it in a more systematic and extended form in the *Critique of Pure Reason*, as his criticism of rational psychology and of rational theology.

as revealed by introspection, but the simplest act of knowledge, that which is involved in all knowledge whatsoever, developed and undeveloped, simple and complex, viz., consciousness of time.[1] That we possess such consciousness, has never been denied by any philosopher, and is, therefore, the really indubitable fact, by the analysis of which Descartes ought to have started. By its actuality it will substantiate the reality of all that can be proved to be its indispensable conditions. This method, which may be regarded as a deepening and correcting of the analytical method of Descartes, is the reverse of Hume's; for instead of setting out, like Hume, from a theory of the ultimate constituents of experience to construct experience, Kant starts from our actual consciousness to discover its conditions. Hume's method is *a priori* and dogmatic, and Kant's alone the truly empirical.

As an illustration of Kant's method we may briefly consider his reply to Hume. Much of Hume's criticism Kant is quite prepared to accept. The general prin-

[1] This is made specially clear in the *Principles of the Understanding* which form the central part of the *Analytic.* Consciousness of time is there taken as the ultimate fact, as conditions of which the objective validity of space and the categories can be established.

ciple of causality is, he agrees, neither intuitively certain nor demonstrable by general reasoning. Like all other synthetic judgments *a priori,* it can only be proved by reference to the contingent fact of our actual experience. Also we can never by analysis of a particular effect discover any reason why it must necessarily be preceded by one particular cause. The nature and possibility of causal connection—the explanation, that is, how one event, the cause, should be able to give rise to another and different event, the effect—is in all cases beyond our powers of comprehension.[1] Yet while admitting the incomprehensibility

---

[1] Cf. *Versuch den Begriff der negativen Grössen in die Weltweisheit einzuführen* (1763) : *Werke,* II. pp. 104-6 :—" I very well understand how a logical consequent flows from its antecedent by the law of identity : an analysis of the antecedent shows it to contain the consequent. . . . But how something follows from something else, and not in virtue of the law of identity, is what I should like to see explained. . . . The former species of ground I term the logical, the latter the real, antecedent. . . . My conclusion is : that the connection between a real antecedent and something which is thereby created or annihilated can never be expressed by a judgment, but only by a conception. No doubt this conception may by analysis be reduced to simpler conceptions of real antecedents : still, after all, our knowledge of this connection always culminates in simple and irreducible conceptions of real antecedents, of which the relation to their consequents can never be made clear." (The above is the translation given by Wallace in his *Kant,* pp. 127 ff.) Cf. *Träume eines Geistersehers : Werke,* II. p. 378.

of causal connection, or, in other words, that it can never be rationalised, Kant establishes against Hume our right to postulate its existence. Consciousness of time is involved in all consciousness whatsoever. And since consciousness of time can be proved to involve, as the condition of its possibility, the consciousness of objects as being all causally connected in space, the principle of causality must have universal validity within our experience. This principle does not, however, carry us very far. Though it justifies us in postulating that for each event a cause must exist among the events immediately preceding, in order to discover what that cause is, we are entirely dependent upon sense-experience.[1] Hume is in the right against the occasionalists. Experience being the sole test of what connections are or are not causal, we must, if experience seems so to indicate, accept any two events, however different, as standing in that relation.[2]

The rationalism of Kant is thus a rationalism of very modest pretensions. It by no means attempts,

[1] The assertion that one particular preceding event is the cause must rest on empirical grounds (such as that it is the only preceding condition which is known to be invariable), and is therefore always liable to be overturned by further experience.

[2] Cf. below, note to p. 260.

like that of Descartes, Spinoza, and Leibniz, to make reality transparent to the mind. As the principles which it establishes are quite formal, though they may suffice to simplify and arrange, they cannot serve either to construct, or to explain, even the simplest phenomena of sense. Also, since those principles are proved only as conditions of our actual experience, and as we can conceive other kinds of experience than that which we possess, besides being limited in their powers of explaining experience, they are further limited to experience. They must never be used (and here again Kant is in agreement with Hume) as instruments for the metaphysical explanation of our experience.[1]

But Kant did not at once manage to fulfil the demands of his own method, and his first position, which is also in great part his last, is itself dogmatic. He adopts the sensationalistic view of the materials of knowledge as consisting of atomic sensations, and recognising the impossibility of deriving space, time,

[1] The physiological explanation of the origin of knowledge must therefore be rejected. Causal connections between mental states and brain-states must, on Kant's principles just as on those of Hume, be accepted as actual; but such connections between particular elements within our experience yield no proof of the existence of conditions outside experience determining it to be what it is.

and the categories, from such data, he asserts, as the sole remaining alternative, that they are supplied by the mind—the mind being conceived in the Cartesian manner as a separate entity, preceding knowledge and rendering it possible. This position, crude though it be, is (thanks to Hume) at least free from the worst defects of the Cartesian rationalism. The innate ideas that on Descartes' view are the God-given means of knowledge of ultimate reality, are for Kant empty forms, of use only for application to the matter of sense. Since the distinction between sense and thought is not a distinction between two kinds of knowledge, but between two elements involved in all knowledge, there can be no purely conceptual thinking. The empiricism of Hume and the rationalism of Leibniz must be regarded as supplementing and limiting one another. In all other respects, however, Kant's position closely resembles the subjective idealism of Locke and Berkeley. Each individual constructs out of given sensations according to inborn laws a subjective world, the objectively real being that which under the same circumstances appears the same to all minds similarly constituted. The understanding, Kant says, creates nature; and each individual creates it anew, he might have added, in his own individual mind.[1] " All objects without exception with which we busy ourselves are in me—that is, are determinations or modes of my identical self." [2]

Now, though not explicitly withdrawing from that position, Kant yet points the way in the ' Objective Deduction ' of the categories to a much deeper one,

---

[1] Knowledge is explained as resulting from the superinduction upon relationless impressions of the rational forms of thought, the superinduction being due to an active self, whose existence is supposed to be ' transcendentally ' proved by its indispensableness for this impossible function. In so far as that is Kant's position we must regard it as a step backward into pre-Humian illusions and not by any means an advance. As the self which Kant here postulates is the occult Cartesian self, he is making use of means that Hume saw clearly to be illegitimate. All that Kant really establishes is the necessity of ' synthesis,' that is, of that unity in experience which is required to render consciousness of time, with all that it involves, possible. But how such synthesis is brought about (if indeed it requires to be brought about), we cannot by general metaphysical reasoning decide. Should synthesis according to the categories be proved not to be due to the direct activity of a noumenal self, but to be the outcome of complex associative processes, such proof would in no wise nullify Kant's conclusions. The self may be, for all that Kant shows to the contrary, not a prior-existing agent that constructs its own experience, but, as Hume urges, the resultant of a preceding complexity of conditions. That, indeed, Kant virtually proves, as we shall see immediately, when he shows that only in and through a complex objective experience is self-consciousness possible.

[2] *Werke*, III. p. 585. This passage was omitted in the second edition of the *Critique*.

that is inconsistent with it. Passing from the problem, how consciousness of objects distinct from the self is possible, to the question how self-consciousness is possible, he discovers that this objective experience, which the self is supposed to create, conditions the very existence of the self. Since the self can only exist as a *conscious* being, and as all consciousness involves consciousness of objects, it is as true to assert that nature makes the self possible, as that the understanding creates nature. Self and not-self presupposing one another, neither can precede the other, so as to render it possible. Experience in its totality, as the unity of self and not-self, is undoubtedly conditioned by the non-phenomenal; but since the manifold of sense and the forms of thought are elements that involve one another, and that cannot even be conceived apart, there is no sufficient reason for the assumption of a noumenal self and of a noumenal not-self as their separate sources. The materialistic and the spiritualistic explanations of knowledge, even when thus combined, are alike illusory.

In the end, therefore, the only attitude which Kant justifies towards experience is the purely

analytical one, which results in a higher empiricism. Without making any assumptions, we
must start from an analysis of actual experience,
and when we do so we find, Kant shows, that it
is made up of qualitatively distinct elements in
necessary interconnection in the homogeneous forms
of space and time; that however far back we
may trace it, both these elements of content and
form are found mutually to involve one another;
and that no explanation can be given how this
experience came into existence, or what are the
conditions beyond it, determining it to be what it
is. Sense-experience, thus constituted, is the whole
sphere of knowledge, and of those realities of
which we have no sense-experience nothing can
be discovered. As all 'necessary' connections are
synthetic, and so *de facto* in their necessity,[1] where

---

[1] Cf. *Kritik der reinen Vernunft: Werke,* III. pp. 150-3.
Mathematical knowledge rests on intuition or sense-perception, and it is because such intuition takes place within a
datum that is from its very nature constant and uniform for all
possible experience (homogeneity and continuity being the
fundamental characteristics of space and of time), that though
the connections which it reveals are, like all other real
connections, synthetic, they can yet be asserted to hold with
universal validity. Kant still claims that some truths
are purely analytic, and therefore are justified by the law
of identity. Such teaching, however, is merely a survival of

sense fails to yield reality, thought must cease to yield truth.[1]

Such are Kant's final conclusions in the *Critique*, and by them the transition is at last made quite out beyond one and all of the Cartesian assumptions. Since consciousness of time involves consciousness of objects interconnected in space, so far is it from being true that we can only be conscious of subjective states, that on the contrary, we can never be conscious of anything purely subjective. The distinction between self and not-self, between inner and outer, is not a distinction between our experience and what lies outside it, but a purely relative distinction within the unity of our objective experience. Our knowledge of external objects is as

his earlier views, and being inconsistent with his fundamental principles may be ignored.

[1] In the *Prolegomena* Kant formulates the fundamental principle of his philosophy in a way that brings out in a striking manner his agreement with Hume in opposition to Descartes. "The principle of all genuine Idealists, from the Eleatic school to Bishop Berkeley, is contained in this formula: 'All knowledge by sense and experience is nothing but mere appearance, and truth is to be found only in the ideas of pure understanding and reason.' The principle which throughout governs and determines my Idealism is: 'All knowledge of things from pure understanding or pure reason is nothing but mere appearance, and truth is to be found only in experience'": *Werke*, IV. p. 121.

certain and immediate as that of our own thoughts. From these results, in the light of which Kant's own philosophy requires to be almost as radically transformed as does that of Hume, modern philosophy makes a fresh start.

INDEX.

of extension, 36 note : his interpretation of the *Cogito*, 50 note :
his proofs that the nature of the
self is not known, 97 ff. : even
the self's existence not known
but only felt, 97 note : that the
essences of things are indivisible,
everything either a substance or
the modification of a substance,
61 note : on perception of figure
and on the relation of figure to
extension, 68 note 2 : on the
laws of motion, 74 note 2 : his
views on mechanical causation
and his occasionalism, 85-7,
197-8, 226-31, 241 note 2, 111
note : his criticism of Descartes'
view of mind and of its relation
to intelligible space, 92 ff. :
secondary qualities all relationless, 94-5, 182 : that we know
space by participation in God's
knowledge of it, 96 note 3 : asserts
the possibility of a rational deductive science of mind, 101-7 :
is one of the founders of empirical psychology, 103 note 1,
188 : asserts the possible modes
of mind to be unlimited in
number, 103 note 2, 194 : from
our knowledge of extension
derives all knowledge of mind,
105 note : his objections to Descartes' doctrine of innate ideas,
109 note 2 : that will is not
essential to mind, 111 note :
that consciousness of being is
prior to consciousness of any par-

ticular form of being, 134-5 : his
influence on Locke, 197-8 : his
views on the causal relation
developed by Hume, 226-31 :
his spiritualism criticised by
Hume, 231 ff. : on creation and
causation, his agnostic conclusion, 241 note 2.

Matter, Descartes' theory of, 65 ff.,
117 ff. : criticisms of his theory,
65-8 : his view of matter raises
new problems as to sense-perception, 15 ff.

Mechanical causation is inexplicable on Cartesian principles,
71-2. See Causation.

Method, according to Descartes
there is one universal method,
22 : why the problem of method
is so important for Descartes,
23-6 : his method in its relation
to the analytical method of the
Greeks, 24 : the characteristics
of the mathematical method, 27 ;
Descartes' criticism of the
empirical method of Bacon, 27-8 :
Descartes' method not syllogistic, 28 ff. : he seeks to make
science purely conceptual,
39 ff. ; contrast between Descartes' method in science and in
metaphysics, 39 ff. : Spinoza's
doctrine of method, 144 ff. :
Spinoza fails to carry out his
method, 153 ff. : Locke's intro-
spective method, 188 : Locke
asserts a two-fold method to be
necessary, 201 ff. : Kant's criti-

SE

h